Reincarnation

Reincarnation

A Christian Perspective

FRIEDRICH RITTELMEYER

Floris Books

Translated by M.L. Mitchell
Revised by Christian Maclean

First published in German under the title *Wiederverkörperung
im Lichte des Denkens, der Religion, der Moral* by Verlag der
Christengemeinschaft, Stuttgart, 1931. First published in English
in 1933 by the Christian Community Press, London. Reprinted with
a foreword by Stewart C. Easton in 1988 by Floris Books, Edinburgh
Third edition 2018

MIX
Paper from
responsible sources
FSC www.fsc.org FSC® C013056

British Library CIP available
ISBN 978-178250-474-0
Printed in Great Britain
by TJ International

Contents

Foreword

It is now over fifty years since Dr Rittelmeyer wrote this book, but it seems to me astonishingly fresh, addressing itself perhaps even more to our concerns in 1988 than it did when it was first published by the Christian Community Press in an English translation. I admired the book when I read it many years ago, and gave it a strong recommendation in my *Man and World in the Light of Anthroposophy*. It seemed to me to be the best book available on the subject of reincarnation, giving the most cogent arguments for its acceptance not only by those who can no longer believe in Christianity and have long ago abandoned it, but equally by believing and practising Christians.

Rittelmeyer himself, who was a well-known Protestant pastor and theologian before he ever heard of Rudolf Steiner, was, as he tells us, always a devout and convinced Christian, and of course remained so until the end of his life. He was also a firm opponent of reincarnation as a non-Christian teaching until he met Steiner, whose teachings on reincarnation showed him that when properly understood it could deepen and clarify his own understanding of Christianity. In the end he came to recognize that only through the knowledge of reincarnation and its incorporation into Christian theology did Christianity itself have a future as a religion that could appeal to every thinking person.

I stress the word 'thinking' here because in the years that have passed since Rittelmeyer wrote his book there has been an immense recrudescence of what one can only call bibliolatry. Numerous sects have proliferated in these fifty years, all taking the Bible absolutely literally as if every word was indeed inspired, and as if nothing except what appears in it has any relevance to Christianity – though of course these sects interpret the Bible as they wish, and emphasize only what seems good to them. On the other hand thousands, possibly millions of people who are neither believing nor practising Christians believe in reincarnation, almost all without taking any great trouble to try to understand what their beliefs involve, and with only the remotest idea of karma, inseparable as it is from any true understanding of reincarnation. Mediums and other 'psychics' claim to be able to tell us who we were in our former incarnations, too often pandering to our human frailties, our self-love, or even our simple curiosity, obviously ignorant of or disbelieving what Steiner says about the extreme difficulty of spiritual investigation in this realm.

Yet Steiner does say that the time is rapidly approaching when many human beings will be born with true intuitions of who they were in former lives, and many more will be oppressed by the karma which they have brought with them without any actual knowledge either of it or who they have been in former lives on earth. One of the great merits of Rittelmeyer's book is its deep seriousness, combined with a sense of profound responsibility towards everything he says. This *is* a subject requiring our most serious and earnest thought, and one cannot help thinking that the enemies of mankind are fully aware of this and for this reason are doing their best to trivialize it, to persuade us that it is something that may be legitimately discussed, as Steiner would have said, at tea-parties, where everyone has something to contribute, but no one has any real idea of what is being talked about, or anything serious to say on the subject.

Rittelmeyer starts his book with an appeal to the reader's capacity for thought. All of this section, the longest in the book, is drawn from anthroposophy. In it he goes carefully into the question of how reincarnation is possible and what is involved in it, the nature of the soul and how it is to be distinguished from the spirit, of life between death and rebirth and the like. All this is beautifully done, and it lays a basis for what he is to say later in the rest of the book on religion and ethics. His aim is not so much to convince as to show how reincarnation, if properly understood, 'makes sense'. But it is in the other two sections that to my mind he is most convincing. *If* one accepts in one's mind the truth of reincarnation, does not this contradict not only the traditional teaching of the resurrection of the body followed by eternal blessedness in heaven or eternal damnation in hell, but also the Bible itself, especially the teachings of St Paul?

Rittelmeyer confronts this difficulty head on. Not only does he state forthrightly that reincarnation is *not* a biblical teaching, but, contrary even to Steiner, who cites the healing of the man born blind as a clear reference by Christ Jesus to the truth of reincarnation,* he rejects or gives other explanations for all those passages where it has sometimes been thought there is a veiled reference to reincarnation. Rittelmeyer does not believe that even the early Christian writers who have sometimes been cited in support of the doctrine ever really accepted, much less understood it. Instead of trying to show that the biblical writers knew about reincarnation but veiled their knowledge, he goes

---

* *The Gospel of St John and its Relation to the Other Gospels,* Anthroposophic Press, USA 1982.

into considerable detail in explaining why it was *not* a traditional Christian teaching, and why this knowledge had to be concealed from mankind until the coming of the consciousness soul.

The knowledge has now in our time become necessary; and Christianity, in Rittelmeyer's belief, cannot survive without it. Clearly he is expressing in this wonderful second section of his book the process of how he himself came to accept this fact once Steiner had given him the necessary indications.

I personally found these pages not only deeply moving, as in the passage concerning kama loca, the Last Judgement and the action of divine grace, but also marvellously convincing, leaving the reader with scarcely an argument left. For this reason, if for no other I would recommend this book as being, of all the works I know, the most suitable for those serious Christians to whose minds the logic of reincarnation appeals, though they continue to have enormous difficulties in reconciling it with what they have been taught since childhood and what they have understood from their reading of the Bible. And those who believe in reincarnation and *for that reason* reject traditional Christianity might well return to it, if with the aid of Friedrich Rittelmeyer they could come to see what a tremendous new understanding both of their own lives and the role of the Christ in human evolution they would gain. They might also recognize why the truth of reincarnation and karma (the latter incidentally scarcely referred to at all by Rittelmeyer, at least overtly) need now to be known and understood if we are to make any kind of moral progress in the centuries to come.

The last section on ethics could, in my opinion, hardly be bettered in a relatively short work of this kind, and shows clear evidence of the author's long experience as a pastor and helper of human souls, both as an Evangelical

Protestant clergyman, and later as founder of The Christian Community. The delicate way in which he speaks of suicide in the light of reincarnation, and of marriage and divorce, again evidence his deep seriousness, and his awareness of problems that today are even more evident than in the 1930s. Nothing that he wrote then is not just as relevant but even more relevant now at the end of the 1980s. Gently he leads us through the thicket of problems and pseudo-problems that beset us in our present age, dealing forthrightly and clearly with possible objections to what he has to say, making clear why a purely hedonistic view of life is or ought to be unacceptable to thinking human beings, and how even the pursuit of personal perfection contains a concealed egotism and cannot be in accord with the divinely willed ordering of the world of which Rittelmeyer is so eminently aware and which he explains so lucidly throughout his book.

The republication of Rittelmeyer's book could not therefore have been more timely than it is now, and it is my earnest hope that it will find many readers and be of help, not only to many serious Christians who are in danger of turning away from their religion because it no longer makes sense to their questing minds, but to those who are more than willing in this age of the consciousness soul to accept reincarnation but have never seriously thought about all its consequences – least of all how it affects all those ethical questions that Dr Rittelmeyer deals with so subtly and beautifully, and, if I am any judge of the matter, so convincingly.

Stewart C. Easton*

* Stewart C. Easton (1907–1989) was a prolific writer on history and anthroposophy. Born in England, he spent most of his working life in Canada and the United States.

Introduction

The author of this book has been brought by destiny into connection with the teaching of reincarnation. He was led by a happy fate to read a history of the world for the first time while still a child of about nine years old. Amid surroundings in which quite different opinions were held, there arose in the youthful mind, which still knew little of the views of the age, the certainty that a human being is not in the world for the first time, that he has himself a connection through an earlier life with mankind's past. This impression rushing up from the depths of his being, returned to him again and again upon different occasions. It was chiefly concerned, not with personalities, but with periods, with whole complexes of feelings, mental gifts, moods. Such experiences, which psychoanalysis does not explain, continued until his twenty-first year, without arousing special vanity or excitement. Then with unexpected force, the consciousness came that he was actively connected with a definite period in the history of Christianity. Thus the idea of reincarnation must have already become a burning problem for him.

But from that point it fell completely into the background. The consciousness of the age demanded more and more of his mind, and filled him with views and thoughts in which the idea of reincarnation had no chance to live.

But it seems as if a subterranean approach to it had still

remained. For in the year 1910, the author wrote a treatise on the doctrine of the transmigration of souls, in which he weighed the pros and cons, recognised much of value in it, but finally rejected it. Immediately after that he became acquainted with the teaching of reincarnation in the form which it takes in anthroposophical spiritual investigation; and now it appeared that no single one of his objections was apposite when brought against that form of teaching. In these circumstances the author may be correct in recognising a dispensation of destiny, and also a duty which he owes to life.

The first conversation which he had with the refounder of the teaching of reincarnation, Rudolf Steiner, turned immediately to this question. 'No, reincarnation is not a doctrine of Christianity,' Rudolf Steiner admitted at once, 'but it is a result of investigation with which Christianity must reckon.' The rest of the conversation, which we shall not discuss in detail here, went in that direction.

So, in this book, we dedicate the first section to a purely intellectual discussion of the idea of reincarnation. Those who have a knowledge of anthroposophical views will naturally find in this part chiefly a presentation of that which is sufficiently known to them already. But the book is intended for those for whom the thought of reincarnation is still a problem with which they are struggling.

The discussion from the Christian point of view is almost entirely confined to the second section, so that all those who find that this method of discussion does not essentially predispose them to accept the thought, may draw near to the teaching of reincarnation by other paths. The author feels this discussion to be a duty for him because he himself from youth up has known Christian circles and their views, and has dedicated his life to the advocacy of Christianity.

The third section is intended to show from the problems

of our life today, the necessity for paying the most serious attention to this question.

As it is possible to be convinced of reincarnation without being a Christian, so it is quite possible to be a Christian without holding the teaching of reincarnation. The contact with Christ which is the cardinal point in Christianity has little or nothing to do with individual questions in one's view of the world, however important they may be. Thus in The Christian Community, to whose public representatives the author belongs, a Christian life may freely unfold itself and be lived out without any reference to reincarnation. The sacramental rituals in which is expressed the spiritual activity that unites The Christian Community make no mention of reincarnation. It can, however, only be said that The Christian Community is the first Christian fellowship within which the thought of reincarnation can be freely entertained, but always as a personal view and confession. This book has been written in this sense, as a free upholding of a personal conviction.

Reincarnation in the Light of Thought

The idea of reincarnation proclaims itself in the west more and more insistently. Theatre dallies with it. Poets dream of it. It peeps unexpectedly out of novels and intimate confessions. It is written about in popular pamphlets.

Have we a new fashionable craze here? Does Europe, as she grows old, seek to forget her need in the illusion of spiritual trifling? Have people, in their lust for sensation, fallen into the strange absurdities of Indian phantasies?

Individuals like Arthur Schopenhauer and Richard Wagner, drawn towards the riddles of the newly discovered wonderland of India, would perhaps not have become such resolved protagonists of the ideas of reincarnation without India. But their standing is too high in the eyes of western society to simply ignore the deepest view they took of life. In them the thought of reincarnation found a form of expression peculiar to themselves.

Yet it can be shown that, even before the discovery of India, the idea of reincarnation arose quite of itself in German cultural life – at the very time when that cultural life freed itself from its Roman wrappings. The arising of the thought of reincarnation in the great minds of Central European culture is one of the most interesting revelations of those underground depths of the soul to which little attention is paid. The number of examples given in

Emil Bock's work on reincarnation is surprising. The idea emerges now here, now there – but never finds the possibility of becoming part of the prevalent ideas of the time. For basically the conception of body and soul had already come into the grip of modern materialism, even where people were still following the banner of idealism. There simply was no possibility of thinking that the soul could wander through several lives. Its connection with the body came more and more strongly into the forefront. People at the highest levels of intellectual life still keenly felt the value of the soul. They denied its transitoriness and inwardly held to and supported themselves by the thought of 'immortality'. But under the onslaught of experiences of the sense world, this inward feeling is becoming weaker and weaker, and the possibility of thinking of the continued existence of the soul within the scientific picture of the world today becomes smaller and smaller.

Thus, as we look at the whole life of today, we find that the hope of existence beyond the grave is lost in odd corners where it is asserted ever more forcefully. In the last resort there remains only the vague hope of continuing to exert some influence the earthly sphere – or some desperate 'And yet!' If this is true for every hope of immortality, it is still more true for such a special idea as that of reincarnation. And therefore the idea of reincarnation, even when it stirs anew in the most sensitive souls, remains fanciful and dreamlike. At best, the breath of a special mood wafts over life.

Although we do not intend here to support our argument by history, yet a glance at the peculiar way in which the idea of reincarnation came to life in Lessing and in Goethe is significant for the further development of our study.

Lessing and Goethe

Gotthold Ephraim Lessing is, as ever, especially instructive. It appears to him unreasonable that a person should touch the earth at one single time only, and in limited circumstances, when the earth with her manifold civilisations has so much to offer, and when their own human talents urge them to such a many-sided development. Such a thought would naturally have weight only if one is convinced that there is a reasonable mind behind the events of this world, and thinks that one can see clearly this mind's intention in the evolving of the individual, and not only in the evolution of civilisation. Belief in a divine goodness which wills to lead people upwards, and to endow them with all its rich gifts, here peeps out of the background.

Two things are clear. Firstly, this thought could be conceived in this form only in the development of western Christian countries. And secondly, from the very first the thought of reincarnation takes on a new form in the western Christian realm of the spirit. In ancient India, no one thought of an 'eternal reason' when they spoke of innumerable reincarnations. They saw themselves brought up against a stern natural destiny in which, if a judgement had to be passed upon it, they perceived rather the eternal unreason of earthly existence. It was no favour of divine love, no felicity for people, that they were tossed from birth to birth, but a gloomy destiny from which they sought release by summoning up all their powers, like seeking to release themselves from the chains of a frightful dungeon. We recognise immediately in Lessing how the idea of reincarnation enters into the mood of the culture of that age which rejoiced in this world here, how the lights of the optimism and rationalism of that day played upon it. But still we have a remarkable indication of the will of the idea of reincarnation to be born again out of Christian convictions about life.

Goethe is quite different. Here we have not the thinking mind which reaches out beyond the one life, and is conscious that it thinks with an eternal reason. Here is the human personality, the human self, which looks beyond the one bodily mantle in which it now finds itself. It has a strong presentiment that it is itself a super-personal self or 'I', which strides forward through the ages. When Goethe looks back at his meeting with Frau von Stein, when he perceives the love of ancient Greece within his soul, then a hidden self begins to stir and burst the bonds of the present. This process in the soul is also radically different from all that has to do with India. It is just this self, this 'I', passing on through the incarnations, which Buddha himself denies. It is a complex of causes, which passes over from one life into another. None of us can now experience in its full strength how mightily and impersonally the people of ancient India felt this human destiny.

What we see before us in Goethe is again a spiritual event in the history of western Christianity, the independence and the significance of which has not yet been sufficiently observed. The human 'I', not only in its value, not only in its strength, not only in its meaning, but simply in its *being* is felt quite differently from the way in which it is felt in India. And out of it arises the idea of reincarnation in a new form. But again this form of the experiencing of the 'I' has arisen upon Christian soil.

Thus we see two characteristic and, at the same time, characteristically different forms of spirit shaping themselves in Lessing and in Goethe, as, without any connection with India, an impulse arises from western Christian circles of culture towards thoughts of reincarnation. Since here we find a groping for the idea of reincarnation, on the one hand out of objective thought about the world, and on the other out of a subjective consciousness of self, we are given significant indications of the future course of spiritual evolution.

Herder

Simply for the sake of the phenomenon, which is so interesting, let us here point to a third spirit among the German classical writers, to Johann Gottfried Herder. One may regard him as a cultivated thinker who, when he perceived its first traces in German cultural life, came forward with the strong intellectual weapons to oppose the idea of reincarnation.

He has a caricature of it before him when he opposes the transmigration of souls in his *Conversations about Metempsychosis*. Yet as one traces the agitation of his spirit more deeply, one discovers that nowhere does he speak more vehemently than when he allows the idea of reincarnation to speak for itself.

> Do you not know any great and unusual people
> who could not possibly have become what they are
> in one single human existence? Who must often
> have been here, so as to have attained to that purity
> of feeling, that instinctive passion for all that is true,
> good and beautiful, in short, to that eminence and
> natural lordship over all that is about them ...
>
> Did not these great people usually appear suddenly?
> Like a cloud of heavenly spirits they descended, as if
> resurrected and reborn, bringing again a new age,
> after a long night of sleep.

Here Herder reaches poetical heights. Something within him unites itself in sympathy with the opponent, whilst he fights against him. The impression made by such descriptions are stronger than the impression given by his intellectual proofs. We should heed such phenomena.

And yet at first German spiritual life got no further than surmises and beginnings. Broad and mighty, the age of natural science arose, and the minds of humanity pressed on optimistically into their investigations in the wide fields offered for conquest. The chief interest, the chief powers of humanity belonged for decades to Nature and her undiscovered kingdoms. The great intellectual achievements which were accomplished there have earned their praise and do not require our acknowledgments.

Rudolf Steiner

But one event was overlooked during this time – an occurrence which broke into the age of natural science and introduced a new age. That occurrence was Rudolf Steiner. His spiritual act was the raising of natural science to a science of the spirit, by which means it again became possible to form a connection with the great spiritual age of a century before.

It is necessary to say this at the beginning, because in the spiritual situation at this point in history the idea of reincarnation can only hope to make its way in intellectual life through the personal. The personality does not matter; it is the spiritual act which is important. No man has spoken more understandingly of natural science than did Rudolf Steiner. Its self-denying methods of investigation, its careful conscientiousness, its intellectual rigour, its valiant precision, he held to be all-important conquests made by humanity which must under no circumstances be lost when new ages arise. Clothed in this armour, which he himself knew so well how to wear in the sphere of natural science, he pressed on into the invisible spheres of the spirit. He was the first real investigator – not merely the surmiser, not merely the believer, not merely the spectator, not merely the thinker, but the first really great investigator – in a kingdom which now really lies before us conspicuous and undiscovered: the kingdom of the spiritual world. It is only because of his surpassing greatness that we have no measure for him; we have not yet got him into true perspective.

Thus the significance of Rudolf Steiner is epoch-making in the history of the idea of reincarnation. Through him it has become possible for the first time to form such conceptions of the relation of body to soul, of life here to the life beyond, of death to life, that the thought of reincarnation has a secure position in human thoughts. The thought of reincarnation is no longer a dream of the soul rising out of unfathomed depths; no longer an idea which was held by ancient humanity and brings a new life of illusion, perhaps only by means of sensation and suggestion; no longer a hypothesis by which people ensure for themselves their own high worth. The thought of reincarnation is rather a self-evident part of a complete view of the world formed by one who has learned to think more spiritually about everything in the world.

If we now have the courage to show the idea of reincarnation in such a connection, what follows may serve to prove whether we have a right to use such words.

The nature of life and death

First we will describe the processes in the soul which lead to reincarnation. Here we may well feel reminded of similar descriptions which one can find in popular occult writings, in the proclamation of mediums, or in documents of the past. What is brought forward here is distinguished from them not so much by the individual results, as by the methods. Nothing is brought forward which has not been independently investigated and carefully tested in detail by an anthroposophical science of the spirit (which means in the first place by Rudolf Steiner). Those who wish at the outset to bring all possible doubts into the field against this assertion, cannot be hindered from doing so. But they may be convinced if they go into the whole presentation of the subject, firstly by the nature of the presentation which is different from the usual accounts of occultism, also by the inward harmony of the whole conception in itself, and lastly by its new relationship to the investigations of natural science.

We begin with the moment of death. What happens then? In earlier ages it was said, 'The soul leaves the body.' All sorts of marvellous opinions, which are incomprehensible today, were current – that the soul floated away like a bird, perhaps through the mouth, and so on. Science today can only say, 'The heart and lungs stop. The life-functions cease to be performed. The body begins to decay.' Naturally there is no doubt of this. The only question is *why* this happens, and whether there is nothing *further* to be said. The actual facts do not prove that 'life' ceases, but only, strictly taken, that a certain kind of life in the *body* ceases, that 'life' leaves the body. What is this life? How could it leave the body? Where does it go? A 'science' which is really exact leaves open the possibility for such questions. It simply says something about the physical body. It takes only into consideration what is visible to the physical eye. But the passing from life to death is entirely mysterious, and quite different from a machine's change from moving to stopping.

How can we get beyond this place at which we are left by the scientific investigation which is tied to observation by the senses, and can tell us no more. We reject the answers offered to us by mediums in spiritualist seances. They may contain correct facts, especially when they agree and are given independently, uninfluenced by one another. But we have no means of testing them. We can best catch a glimpse of the unknown if we observe more closely the last moments of the dying.

The panorama at the moment of death

It is known that in a moment of deadly peril, in falling from a height or in drowning, many people see wonderful pictures of their past life arising before them. In the course of my life I have heard about twenty people describe this experience in different and yet in similar forms. These people for the most part knew nothing about anthroposophy. The past stood before them, either in single scenes, or in tableaux of a period, or in a panorama, more clearly, and especially more arrestingly and more vividly, than in the usual memory pictures. These people described especially the objectivity of the impressions and their rapid sequence in which all the usual means of measuring time were useless. I read of such an experience for the first time in a daily paper, about thirty years ago. A doctor described what took place within him from the moment when the bullet fired by an opponent in a duel hit him till the moment when he fell and lost consciousness. He himself, a materialistic man of science, declared that he could not imagine a life after death. But the experience was so overwhelming that he felt it a duty to describe it to his fellow human beings.

In a later case a student, who had been an airman in the war, told me that during a high fever he had seen pictures of how artillery fire directed by him penetrated the enemy's trenches. He had before him not only what he himself had done, but also the consequences of it for others, against whom his acts were directed. His experience was so depressing, that he sought help. In a clarity which is scarcely known in ordinary daily life, with a swiftness which covers an age in a second, the past sped before him. What is this phenomenon?

The first answer which we receive is 'the subconscious mind'. What has been stored 'down there' can in moments of strong emotion rise up into the consciousness. This 'subconscious mind' cannot be denied. But it cannot be said that in talking about it we are expressing anything essential, or solving or even touching upon any problem whatsoever. The 'subconscious' is merely a word. It is even merely a denial – a denial of consciousness. But it denies 'subconsciously' much more than it ought to deny. According to that, at least one must also assume that this 'subconscious mind' for example must also cease to exist when consciousness is extinguished in death. But then one also assumes that this subconsciousness cannot also have *its* consciousness which for once pushes itself forward. And one also assumes that in general there is only one form of consciousness namely the form known until now – day consciousness. For one seldom dares to speak of a consciousness in the subconsciousness.

One finds plentiful groups of mistakes like these in one-sided materialistic investigations. How is this 'subconscious mind' retained within man? Only by the structure of the body? Has it its own 'principle of organisation' within the body, or near the body, or above the body? How is the whole texture, if one may use this term, interwoven? Are there upper layers? Under what conditions does it emerge 'into consciousness'? To say 'excitement' is to say little. What independence can this 'subconscious mind' acquire? What action, what continuance is possible for it after death? One is seldom aware that all these are still open questions; that one can conceal these open questions from oneself by words, which one has formed for oneself provisionally and perhaps too hastily. The method of investigation used by natural science today regarding the life of the soul, resembles an angler who sits upon the seashore and waits for what chance may bring him. In comparison with the man who goes for a walk, the angler has a longer rod and can reach further out. He has some thoughts which he has formed for himself as he sat and fished. But he does not even have a boat with which to put out upon the sea, let alone diving apparatus with which to see into the depths. And out there, wave ever following wave to break upon the shore – there is the sea!

Those who bring this into their 'consciousness' would have sufficient reason to listen attentively to what is said about the sea out of other methods of investigation. They would then perhaps understand better what they themselves catches with their hook.

The etheric

That which permeates the body and gives it life, is, according to anthroposophical investigation, not an abstract 'force' which breaks in out of the void when the physical conditions are fulfilled, but an organism of forces whose vehicle is a fine substance which can no longer be perceived with the earthly eyes. Natural science, it is true, also finds itself compelled to assume a kind of 'ether' as such a vehicle for the action of forces. Only it is in danger – because it can approach the ether only tentatively from the side of observation by the senses – of forming its conceptions of the ether from the physical side and so, perhaps, of grasping only one side of the truth, and perhaps not even that correctly. No one has yet seen the ether of physicists. The organ of perception for this 'substance' is not the physical eye, but one of these higher faculties which are described in the book *Knowledge of the Higher Worlds*. If one has gained definite impressions of these higher organs of perception at any point, one knows certainly that here great undiscovered wealth lies waiting for mankind.

Another possibility of perceiving the 'etheric', at least in oneself, is found in meditation, when the capacity to distinguish what belongs to the soul, both from the physical and in itself, has reached a certain stage. For the investigator who will not or cannot go along this way, the 'etheric' remains a hypothesis, a useful assumption, whether in the sense of natural science or in the sense of a science of the spirit, but still it can acquire from thinking a great probability. And we can ask which of the two points of view explains the external facts themselves more illuminatingly and comprehensively.

If we call the organisation of forces which permeates human beings and makes them alive during the period of their life, the 'etheric body', we must constantly bear in mind that we are using neither the word 'ether' nor the word 'body' in its usual sense. Such a body is not something visible in the physical sense, and such an 'ether' is not anything physical in the hypothetical sense. If we cannot retain this in our mind and in our feelings as well, then everywhere misunderstandings will spring up. The misfortune of the words which we must use for spheres of which the majority of people have as yet no experience, will continue with us. But how can we avoid this danger? One can only describe it to readers as exactly as possible and suggest to them that they form an idea of a plane, when up till now they have seen only a car.

All our experiences continually enter into this substance-borne organism of forces, into this 'etheric' body. Therefore those impressions also, upon which the rays of our consciousness have not fallen, may act in such a way as to vitalise or to destroy the organism. In this fine substance not only are the effects of our experiences upon our feelings retained, but also the pictures of these experiences themselves as they have passed through our senses. People always have with them all their experiences, and do not know it. That is why in old age pictures of one's youth arise, to which one has not had access for decades, which one had never suspected were still there. Therefore in the case of an alarming experience such as an assault, experiences arise and surround one like pictures. The etheric body slightly loosening its connection with the physical body, then betrays its secrets. And so people always carry an uncanny possession about with them. Their box of memories may open at any moment. They themselves are a great hoard of memories. They are more; they are above all that which collects and organises these memories. Viewed from above, if one looks away from the physical appearance, they are a wandering remembrance.

Death

When the physical body can no longer be used, then death takes place. That means the etheric body must let go the physical body, must, as it were, let it fall. It can no longer live and work there. And so it separates itself from it. That does not mean that this organism of forces in which the memories have buried themselves immediately disappears out of the world, but it has the tendency to dissolve into the common cosmic ether. That lasts for days, like a cloud-mass gradually becomes more vague in its outlines and dissolves into the surrounding atmosphere. The ordinary cohesion and connection to our body and requires about three days for its dissolution. And the three, or three-and-a-half days, of the mysteries are connected with this fact. In the case of the individual, the length of time is different according to the power of keeping awake that the person had during life. This power of keeping awake also consists in the capacity of the higher human being to retain the life-forces, to press itself close to the life-forces, as it were.

During these three days, the etheric being in which the human being has lived pursues its natural tendency – and the tendency of such life-forces is always to reproduce themselves. During the physical life this tendency was restrained, as the tendency of a tree's life may be checked by a stone which it has to carry. The physical body, with its coarser experiences, with its strong needs, claimed these life-forces for the most part for itself. As if lamed, the impressions of the etheric body sank, at first, into the unconscious. But now their hour has come. What happened earlier occasionally and partially – namely that the etheric pictures stirred within one – happens now all at once of necessity and in completeness. On all sides they flash forth. Spiritual flames flicker round the person. Their whole past life rises up, and they themselves are in the midst. They look themselves in the eye, as they come out of their life to meet themselves. The person judges himself. For this etheric being, which bears within it the pictures of the past life, reveals as it passes into the cosmic ether how the human life itself stands in the higher world.

If one wished, one could say that is the 'technique' of the first judgement, through which man has to pass. But a word like 'technique' would immediately lead one into error. Here we are dealing with a world order, supported by spirits which order it. And the feeling that such living powers are present creates the character and the seriousness of this looking back upon life. Finer senses awaken in a person now when the world of sense sinks from them, leaving them alone in a higher world. For no one 'gives up the ghost', not even the most thorough-going materialist. What the person living most strongly in the senses gives up, must give up, is the body. And then spirit stands before spirit.

If one tests these ideas, and all that is said hereafter, one will nowhere find a point at which the results of natural-scientific investigation are contradicted. Therefore, natural science would on its part have no grounds for contradiction. No one denies the 'excited nerves' of men in peril of death. It is only the web of life as revealed in pictures which appears because of this danger, which we are studying and explaining. What is yet unknown is added to what is known. And it is not asserted that what is added here can be seen with the eye, captured by instruments or be discovered by the intellect. It is absolutely impossible for anyone to have it demonstrated to them unless they are willing to adopt the new methods of investigation. If anyone were to think they could contradict it by other means, they would be like the giant who wished to fight the god Thor on earth, while that god could only be defeated in the air.

The soul

But the soul – so the spiritual investigator tells us – does not take its flight 'into the cosmos' when its etheric dwelling has dissolved itself into the universal etheric. It is rather another connection into which it enters which appears clearly, and is more tenuous and more spiritual. The 'substance' which is now its vehicle – again using the word 'substance' with reserve – is called the 'astral body'. It is 'such stuff as dreams are made on', to use Shakespeare's words. It is connected with the most delicate currents of forces which come down from the stars.

That the life of our soul is influenced by the constellations no one can deny who has heard anything about sleep-walking. As compared with the coarser influence of the weather, such influences upon us are certainly of a more delicate kind. For the most part they remain unconscious. But since they are there, they also require a medium which flows throughout not only the cosmos, but also through human beings, and this medium is called the 'astral being'. In this connection we mention the investigations of Lili Kolisko into the influence of stars on matter; we are again faced with the tragic fact of an investigator pursue their way for years alone, before anyone joins them to test and pursue their work.

Our soul life is related to the stars. Out of the starry spaces the 'stuff' in which it weaves is woven. It does not pass away when the earthly shell is dissolved. Human beings actually raise themselves to the stars. Only one must not form the idea that this happens in space. Just as thoughts which are thought in America, Germany and Russia can flow together into a mighty spiritual movement, so that no railways which run between can restrain it, so the spirituality which is in human beings recognises the spiritual world to which it belongs, and unites itself with it, and is not disturbed by the thousand things which happen in the physical world.

Human beings now live in a much more delicate and more spiritual mode of being, the 'astral being', and within it that which has organised the astral being in this especial way – namely the innermost self, the 'I'. Only now, when we reach this 'I' and this higher spirituality, does it become impossible to speak of 'matter'.

We must become accustomed to this mode of being. We must awake to it. It is no less rich in experiences than the earthly sphere in which the spiritual has support in the earthly world, in the brain; it is even richer, but quite differently, much more 'spiritual' and 'delicate' – there are no other words for it. In such a world all spiritual relationships reveal themselves inescapably to the soul. From this fact flow all the pangs and all the joys of this mode of being. To take an example: if someone has been very susceptible on earth to the pleasures of the table when they were offered, but at the same time could forget all about food when enjoying music – which is a spiritual pleasure – so that only gnawing hunger reminded him of his bodily existence, then such a person would easily grow accustomed to a world in which there were no more dinners. But someone whose chief joy in existence was to look forward to the next meal, who knew nothing higher than a roast; such a person would be destroyed when the soul, which had been intimately interwoven with such joys, found itself in a world where there were no more menus.

Such an example shows to what a large extent the ideas of the life beyond which were held in past ages really mirror the truth. In Greece they spoke of Tantalus in Hades, who was for ever reaching after a fruit which just escaped his grasp. In India, they described in kama loca the karmic results of earthly actions. In the Catholicism of the Middle Ages, we have the representation of the fires of purgatory. Through a dreamy clairvoyance, not through wild fantasy nor capricious conjecture nor through 'speculation', if one understands the word in the sense of 'mirroring', humanity received news of what passes after death. It was described in differing pictures, by peoples and civilisations. But one cannot fail to recognise the typical basic experience. In a spiritual manner, conformable to our way of thinking at the present day, spiritual investigation illuminates what was still perceived by humanity in former ages of the world. The multitude of pictures, even if there is much in it that is confused and disordered, illustrates the restrained account of those matters which we have given. And our thought-perception explains and clears the many-coloured pictures.

The ascent of man is accomplished thus: the lowest desires, which have taken up their abode in the starry being of the soul, must die through lack of satisfaction before the soul can have more peaceful joy in the higher impulses which also dwell in it. Unfulfilled desires burn, as thirst can burn. Through our dreams we know this spiritual burning which can so occupy the soul, that it cannot think of anything higher. This new world is serious enough for all those who have betrayed their souls to earthly pleasures. With their sensitive feelings they must now pay the ransom for this. But souls like Francis of Assisi pass almost untouched through this new world, as they have passed unstained through their temptations upon earth. The fire of purgatory is a crude but not incorrect expression for this world, and only the later dogmatic definition *ignis corporalis et realis* (fire which is bodily and real) lies on the path of materialistic error.

The experience of our life after death

In this time after death human beings wander back through their past life. The spiritual experiences which have been stored up within them are now examined by him, step by step, and are felt in the cosmic astral being where they occupy the place that is fitting for them. Pictures always reveal such experiences most clearly, but they demand of readers that they see through these pictures with their understanding and not with their misunderstanding.

As if with the many eyes of the cosmic powers, which now awaken within us, because like finds like, we look into their life in every way. We 'judge' ourselves, as we are judged by the higher cosmic powers which now, in eternal calm, as inviolable and incorruptible judges, view what is brought before them. We are judged by them, while being judged *according* to them. From there the last judgement comes to us. We bear it always with us in our conscience. By the forces which draw our soul after them, will it be known where it belongs, whether to lower or to higher regions of the cosmos. No brief words of external judgement are spoken, but one relationship of our being after another comes before us, until the soul is 'purified'; that means, till everything in it which can no longer live in the higher air has died. So the soul is drawn higher and higher till it reaches the 'heaven' to which it has destined itself in its earthly life.

The fairy tale of Volkmann-Leander, in which every soul finds just that world it most deeply longed for on earth, is fulfilled, like many another legend of our childhood. Every soul bears irrevocably within it the spiritual forces which draw it upward, because, in its deepest nature, it is from above. But its past earthly life determines how high, how swiftly, how consciously it can enter the higher, the highest worlds, which all lie open for it. An earthly example may make this clearer. Let us assume that a great gathering of people are assembled in a hall where Beethoven's *Ninth Symphony* is being played. What will the effect be? Many 'experience' nothing. The wearisome noise only awakens their impulse to get up and go; more and more insistently and painfully wishes and needs arise within them which Beethoven does not satisfy. Others hear with their ears the highest inspiration of a genius, look into the open heaven, and listen to choirs of angels. No outward sentence is needed to judge between them. The inward preparation each brings declares itself.

Proof and awareness of the spiritual

So human beings rise through innumerable experiences, till their last and highest, *their* last and highest is completely attained. They has found no materialistic paradise, but *their* heaven – not the heaven of which they thought, but the heaven which thought in them. There the soul rests until all are made one.

'And we are supposed to have experienced this already. Many times? This is fantasy run wild! We find no trace of it in our memory! And if it is not in our memory, has it any significance for us? Do we wake up out of such a web of dreams which makes use only of our unconsciousness, and by our unconsciousness of it is again disproved?'

Now, first of all, anyone who thinks that what he does not remember, cannot be within him, has a psychology which can be cured by the most superficial consideration. For that, no psychoanalysis is required. Even the sleep-walker has experiences to which he can find no key in the waking consciousness of day. But every dreamer encounters the same thing. We wake in the middle of the night. It gradually comes into our consciousness that we have been dreaming vividly. But the dream is present with us only as a strong feeling. We can get no access to it. Then after a time it occurs to us, and now, all at once, the dream-picture in all its details comes vividly before our soul. If we pay close attention, we can, in such a moment, study the difference between different forms of consciousness. But that does not yet interest us – not yet. And at night, if we suddenly wake up? Perhaps our dreams were less vivid; but were they not there? Often in the course of the day a dream complex arises instantaneously before us. Perhaps we even become conscious suddenly that we have often dreamt the same dream before, but if there had been no external cause, this dream-complex would not have come to light. It would have remained submerged, but not inactive.

Sometimes we notice, when we observe ourselves, that in our decisions we find the mood of an oppressive dream playing a part – a dream whose details we cannot bring to mind. In every case when we act out of experience a cloud of experiences takes part in our decisions, though they have not passed through the light of our consciousness. Do we require further examples?

'But the difference is that at least occasionally we observe the after-effects of these "unconscious" experiences in our earthly life, but of a "life" in the spiritual world we cannot find the slightest trace!'

That is just the question. Perhaps we are only lacking in observation. Do we not 'instinctively' shrink back from some spheres of experience, from which others do not shrink? Are we not drawn to other spheres by an inexplicable attraction, as if we were 'at home' there? Are not many things 'natural' to us, which are certainly not 'natural' to others? Are we not endowed with capacities upon which we can securely depend? Is it not true that in reference to this or that we need only refresh our memories, while others learn slowly in the sweat of their brows?

'Heredity!' says someone, using the catchword of the moment. Certainly the facts of heredity speak loudly enough. We have no cause to gainsay them. But one question always remains unsolved. What is the organising principle which makes the choice out of the enormous mass of inherited capacities? Is it chance? We shall meet again this question of heredity at a decisive moment when we speak of our birth. Here let us say only that we do not deny any of the results of the science of heredity. But they explain only the substratum, not the subject. How the individual human talents and inclinations are put together – this question remains quite open. If one thinks that here one *could* only consider the blind play of natural forces, one is a materialistic dogmatiser. Chance, like God, is seen by nobody. At this point the science of heredity, after it has upheld all its well-won rights, can only hold its peace, and admit honestly that a question still remains. It can then turn away from all that cannot be proved by the senses, or it can listen to what another science has to say.

If only one could for once make clear to the clever intellectualist of today that the same proofs cannot be given for the invisible side of the case, as for the visible side. To demand them is just as unreasonable, just as foolish scientifically as to require photographs of the spiritual ideas of higher mathematics. One cannot even 'prove America'. Even to the American who comes over here, I can prove, not indeed that there is no America, but that he has not proved and cannot prove America. If I bring only mistrust to the accounts of those who have been over there, no power in the world can convince me. I must myself travel there. I may listen very circumspectly and with reserve, but it may be that the more I listen to those who tell of America, the more I come to have faith in them.

Yet we are not merely thrown back on faith. The more we learn to 'meditate', that means, the more we learn not only to think thoughts in, but to live in the spiritual realm; not only to have sudden ideas and to draw logical consequences, but to experience thoughts with all the force of reality, and let them live themselves out in us; to walk and also to stand still in a world of thought; to pass over into it and place as it were the whole weight of our existence in it – the more we learn in this way to have the whole impression of our soul-being before us at once (and this means to learn and to practice much) then we will see the more clearly what a many-sided, rich, characteristic structure we have before us. We will see more clearly the great weight of our inheritance and within it our 'I', which works and organises it spiritually, and wills to rule over it. And it will be so much the less possible for us to regard this 'I' as the offspring of a union between chance and nought at all.

Therefore, how strong our experience is of the ability to 'look down' from the spirit upon the body is a question of self-training and of nothing else. One may use this expression because the spiritual in the human being is perceived as a separate spiritual element on which influences from the body act, as it were. We then know: here I live purely in the spirit. Then the body stirs with its laws and demands.

We see ourselves as a human individual in a certain stage of development, beneath us is what we have attained, above us that which we have still to attain. We have a vivid feeling that we have set out on a spiritual pilgrimage.

It will never be possible to make anyone believe in such experiences if they have not at least some idea of them. Such methods as Theodor Ziehen uses are no longer applicable. He writes: 'All the assertions of the egotists [who assume that there is an ego] do not enable them to escape this fact, that there are people who declare definitely that they have never had the smallest experience of egotistic intuition.'* The untenability of such proof comes sharply into view if one places this sentence beside his sentence: 'All the assertions of the philosophers do not enable them to escape this fact that there are people who know nothing of pure thought.' Can one then controvert a fact by stating that there are people who have had no experience of it? Is the truth that alone which *all* people have experienced? One can see the state of mind out of which such a failure in thinking proceeds. The self-evident presupposition of the philosopher, though he does not prove it nor does it even enter into his consciousness is this: there can be nothing in the soul of which a mind which lives upon the heights of philosophy has no personal experience.

How much more circumspect and scientific is, for example, Oswald Külpe. He finds that there is a 'right to have a psychological metaphysic'. Whether it will have the character of a 'theory of substantiality' is, of course, 'in no way decided'. 'Scientific psychology is not yet broad enough or ripe enough to enable one to make definite assumptions about the nature of of the soul.'† This is the scientific attitude, which it is

---

* T. Ziehen, *Grundlagen der Psychologie* (Principles of psychology), p. 120.
† O. Külpe, *Einführung in die Philosophie* (Introduction to philosophy), 5th edition, p. 276.

possible to discuss. Really – however much such an assertion may be interpreted as arrogance – it is a concern only of human evolution that the spirit acquires independence of the body, even that the individual spirit acquires it. The turning away of humanity from this upward path, on which in the 'classical age' it had advanced far, has been caused by the one-sided development of the powers of understanding. This was required by the age of natural science. But today it becomes dangerous to the inward and upward evolution of mankind – yet it can also be made serviceable to it. Someone has an idea of the real nobility of humanity only when they are able to live in the spirit, clearly, securely and consciously; when they feels that they are the ruler, or at least the superior of their bodily being. Then the tales of a coming life in the spirit grow more comprehensible and interesting. They come more and more into the illuminated spheres of probability.

Therefore we are not left to learn at death what comes after it. Physiologically we bear about within us the past ages of humanity. That we can also physiologically draw conclusions about the future of the human race from our own bodily circumstances is certain. It is necessary only to have sufficient clearness of spirit. And clairvoyance, in the healthy and correct sense, is nothing but increasing clearness of spirit. So we must have our spiritual future after death already within us in embryo. It would not be *our* future if we could not already overhear its messages within us. For that we do not require spectacles, nor stethoscope nor forceps, but the creating of a state of spirit which is for the most part like the condition which can exist only after death. One cannot establish a theoretical dogmatic proof of what ought to be possible, but can only examine, actively and practically, what is possible.

Experiencing the spiritual world

Let us mention one possible means by which we can come to have ideas of the experiences which we had before birth. Rudolf Steiner has often pointed out how we can go back into our earliest youthful experiences. If we succeed in bringing to life again within us all that we felt about life before we were conscious of ourselves, it will seem to us that then we were enfolded in glorious and golden blessedness. We need only observe those feelings of childhood which we can still recall with a little more exactitude and self-devotion – not merely enjoy the feeling of them, not simply sing them as a poet would, but observe them spiritually and objectively – and we will find that we feel as if we had then descended from heaven to earth. We have a feeling such as we might have on awakening out of deep sleep. It then seems to us as if we were bringing with us to earth delicate forces of joy. Our spirit does not yet penetrate more deeply. In awakening we have the same kind of experience only in a weakened form.

It becomes increasingly difficult to find the explanation of this 'youthful blessedness' simply in the dewy freshness of our physical sensations, or the unexhausted powers of hope in the soul, or in our inexperience carefully guarded at home. It is spiritual, sun-inspired joy which radiates through us, not freshness of body. In this spiritual joy those around us may bathe without our knowing it. Why, at first, does our memory not go further back? Can we marvel at that if we ourselves have such inexact memories when we go back to this time? What if we have forgotten this spiritual, sun-inspired joy in which we then lived, and which gave new life daily to all around us? It is still woven into our life. In old age, and in old age especially, one can often feel the continued working of this warm radiance of childhood.

Let us point out still one more experience. People of past ages have often had it, obviously more vividly than people today. Otherwise Plato could not have said with such enthusiasm that all the great flashes of illumination which came to him were memories. Even among us it happens that a person – an artist for example – goes about as if looking for something which he has lost. To the question how he got his music Anton Bruckner replied, 'I have listened to the angels.' When we open ourselves to his inspired compositions, it seems to us as if he had been listening to a solemn religious service, of which the Catholic mass itself is only a copy. When we listen to Brahms we often feel as if he were seeking some melodic mode of being which shines upon him in brief flashes, but when it does shine opens to him endless perspectives. When we hear Beethoven, it is as if we were present at a storming of heaven by Titans, and then, out of a heaven which has gently opened, the blessed gold of peace descends upon the storming Titans. Such impressions help us to understand the statements of spiritual investigators, that great artists, especially in music, labour to bring into this earthly world something of the harmonies of the spheres in which they lived before birth.

When the human soul has reached the highest spiritual heights which it can then reach, it becomes one with the world in which it now dwells. This has a twofold significance. Its power to rise comes for the time to an end. One may, as a rough comparison, think of an airship whose content of gas cannot raise it higher in the surrounding atmosphere. Such pictures give only bare hints of what is spiritual. But this becoming one with the world is also a going to sleep. We no longer distinguish ourselves from our surroundings, and this distinction no longer comes into our consciousness. A blessed rest in becoming one with the divine world which our soul now reaches is the highest experience to which it attains.

First inklings of return to earth

But then, in the individual core of the soul, the inclination to descend begins to prevail. Not by the laws of nature but by a spiritual attraction, this inclination draws the soul towards the place where it can work and learn, where it can derive a new upward impulse, a new union with the spiritual world. As it now, as it were, sinks slowly towards earth then in all the realms through which it passes in its return course, it incorporates into itself all that is suited to it. From all sides what belongs to its being flows to it and unites itself to it. And so it draws near to physical existence. Now it has to find the body which can serve it. Out of the stream of inheritance an innumerable variety of embryonic bodies is offered to it. And yet, perhaps for decades, it finds no embryo in which it can live. For the embryo of the body also bears within it possibilities which must enter into harmony with the inclinations of the soul. So the soul must wait until somewhere upon the whole earth it can find the embryo body which offers to it the possibilities which it requires.

All this is accomplished one might say, according to natural laws, but then one must bring into a wider connection both these natural laws and *spiritual* ordinances, and must know that 'laws' are never abstract and in the air as materialistic intellectualism is bound to think they are, but they are the modes of action of spiritual powers. When one understands that it may be the same thing to say, 'Souls are guided by natural laws,' as to say, 'Souls are led by angels,' then one approaches the truth which we are describing here.

Even when the soul has found a bodily embryo, that embryo is seldom as well-suited as it would wish it to be – especially seldom in our time. This growing body, in which the powers of inheritance act, often presents great hindrances to the soul. The embryo indeed, is capable of being moulded. The soul can, indeed, through years – beginning before birth, then in other ways after birth up till the third year, then in other ways throughout the whole of life – work upon it in order to make it in an obedient instrument. But the forces of heredity are also at work upon the body, the common human forces, springing from the whole evolution of humanity, as well as the special personal forces from the father and mother. And so even the embryo most akin to the soul, does not offer it some things which it requires, and also offers it some things which it does not require. Feelings of discomfort not seldom accompany the soul throughout life. It feels as if it could not bring to full expression what it wants to express. But just because of the opposition, such a life may grow to so much the greater power for a life which is still far off.

What objections can investigators into heredity make to such a view? No one can say that the actual facts of the science of heredity are robbed of their value if one gives heed to the three results: first, that under certain circumstances for decades the soul does not find what corresponds to its need, although millions of possibilities of life are at its service; secondly, also that no embryo fully corresponds to what the soul requires; and thirdly, that the soul can set strong forces to work in remodelling the growing body from its most tender beginnings. Many crises and illnesses, which cannot rightly be explained, are comprehensible as arising from this struggle between soul and body. One must say that not only has no investigation of heredity up till now been able to discover any definite facts about the organising principle that leads to the coming into existence of any particular person, but also that it will never be able to work out anything about this with its present methods. At this point, the ultimate fact for it would be simply the mechanism of procreation, if one did not see that other methods, which lead to the investigation of that which is living, might be able to help.

One can assert this so definitely because in the most different spheres, science always comes up against the same questions, and can give no answer. What is it which organises? Through what does it work? How does it work? How does it live and die? Nowhere with the present methods of investigation is there even the faintest glimmering of real perception. One can say still more definitely than did those investigators of nature out of their insight *ignoramus – ignorabimus* (we do not know – we shall not know). And science has stood by this confession since Emil du Bois-Reymond made it in 1872 in his lecture on the limits of our knowledge of nature. In this position, science is standing before two doors. She can knock at the door of free speculation or she can knock at the door of higher investigation, whose results she may at first assume hypothetically and hold them along with her own results.

A new light falls on other problems of biology also, besides the problem of the organising principle, through the idea of reincarnation. Let us mention only one. The question is often asked why certain peoples are doomed to extinction. Doctors and biologists have made their investigations. They have found nothing to explain why these peoples are dying out. The processes of life were in order. The bodily organisations of the men and women were healthy. Why is it? Here also the perceptions of a science of the spirit give an answer. There are always fewer and fewer souls which find the conditions necessary to their development in the bodies of these peoples. And therefore the life embryos are not used. Is this fancy? Only for one who absolutely refuses to follow new methods and test them, although the old methods obviously do not lead to the goal, obviously cannot lead to the goal. Is it not crasser fantasy always to imagine that by physics and chemistry in the modern sense, one can approach near to the problem of life?

Examples of reincarnation: Novalis, St Francis

In order to have a picture of how the human 'I' proceeds through the incarnations, we may quote here two of the many examples given by Rudolf Steiner, especially in the last period of his life. They are taken from public lectures or from lectures afterwards made public. We must again emphasise that one would completely misunderstand such communications if one thought that conclusions were drawn here, suppositions brought forward, or that we were being given the fancies of a medium. What is here told claims to have been investigated by exact methods, modelled upon the methods of natural science, but modified to correspond with another sphere of investigation. One may test the exactitude of these methods; one may dispute the correctness of the results, or regard them provisionally as being undecided. But if one has not tested these methods and does not even know them, one cannot out of the blue assert that the results have been obtained by other methods than the investigator himself says they were. Such behaviour would be unscientific.

The first example deals with the connection between Raphael and Novalis. From this example one may see how what is gained in one life becomes active in a new life. Everyone finds it surprising how deep an understanding is found in Novalis for the greatness of an ideal Catholicism, although he lived in another age amidst surroundings quite opposed to it. Especially remarkable are the lines, which however, were not quoted by Rudolf Steiner, and which must not be regarded as the basis of any conclusion:

I see thee in a thousand forms,
O Mary, drawn with loving care,
And yet by none art thou revealed,
As in my soul I find thee there.

I only know that this world's clamour
Has since flowed by me like a dream,
And that a sweet and nameless heaven
Eternal in my mind has been.

What Novalis brought with him was a knowledge of the intellectual depth of Christianity. What he sought was nature, but nature into which he carried his deep consciousness of the spirituality of the world. If one is to show the right scientific spirit, one can only stand thoughtfully before such information given by the spiritual investigator. Behind our usual daily studies, unfathomed depths of life await us.

Measured by the space of time, after which reincarnation usually occurs, the transition from Raphael to Novalis is an unusually early reincarnation. These two personalities are as it were two revelations of the same being, but as it advances in evolving.

The other example leads us into quite a different relationship. Many people have already observed the connection of Francis of Assisi with Buddhism. The author of this book, for example, once proposed to write a book about the union of Christianity and Buddhism in Saint Francis. That gentle love of animals, that love of his holy bride, Lady Poverty, that feeling of unity with all nature, that ready receptivity for all the impressions of life, and with all this, that heroism of ascetic self-denial, and the mood of that final doxology in praise of death the redeemer – how did such a character grow up so suddenly out of Italy of the Middle Ages? If one holds that reincarnation is possible, one will find food for thought in the statement of Rudolf Steiner that, in an earlier incarnation, Francis was a pupil in a school for initiates on the Black Sea, which was under the spiritual influence of Buddha.

The educated person of today is trained to perceive all kinds of feelings which appeal to the senses, but not to observe the more delicate divisions of his soul-life. He can perceive complexes when impressions creep into the unconscious soul-life and grow there like ulcers. But there is little sense awakened in him of how to observe, for example, the way in which, out of the enduring human 'I', something pulses through the manifestations of a life – how this pulsing is now stronger, now weaker: how it is lessened by passing impressions and fancies; how it is almost extinguished by the more persistent habits of life – of the way, in short, in which the 'I' lives in its interplay with the astral and etheric life, which also belongs to it and with which it is in contact. Only when one looks *into* the human being with more delicate observation does one clearly perceive the 'I', which can be distinguished from its sheaths, and which yet imbues them with its own nature and passes through the ages independently, or, rather, ever becoming more independent.

One's own previous life

Rudolf Steiner never spoke of his own incarnations. He completely overcame that temptation – one must add, if indeed for him it was a temptation. Of the ethical greatness of his lifework, mankind in general has not even a suspicion. Whatever was said or thought in the immediate circle around Rudolf Steiner concerning his earlier incarnations rests upon surmises, which are based upon historical associations of facts. Such surmises may hit the mark, but also may often err. That these circles held Rudolf Steiner to be Christ reincarnated or that he ever let himself appear in this light is one of the hundred slanders which tend to obscure his real character. Rudolf Steiner has always emphasised the uniqueness of the Christ as a phenomenon in history. The only statement I myself ever heard from him occurred in an intimate conversation. He said that sometimes from outside something correct might be said to a person concerning that person's past. He himself had been enlightened about his own earlier incarnation by a remark made after a lecture, which set him on the right track. Rudolf Steiner mentioned no name.

Even apart from the restraint which is tactful in such conversations it would have been impossible to question him. He knew how to guide such conversations. I know of no one who would have dared to ask him. Everyone knew too well what they were to expect if they had asked. The single exception which Rudolf Steiner made in speaking of reincarnations is distinctive of his attitude. On their seventieth birthdays, he spoke to a very few of those nearest to him, about their earlier existence. Then no falsifying influence could be exercised upon their lives by such information. And also, in the few cases in which a more explicit word was spoken, it was done in so careful and gentle a way, and so humanly, that one could study in it the art of dealing with people. Such information was never particularly flattering.

This recital may seem to interrupt the course of thought in our study. But through it one may come to feel in what kind of atmosphere Rudolf Steiner investigated and spoke – in what spiritual atmosphere the hope alone rests of reaching truth in this sphere.

Does one then have memories of a past life? Many people in the present assert that they have such memories. If one looks more closely, one finds that they are such impressions as,

'I have been here before,' 'I have been through this already,' or 'I have already met these people.'

One can only utter a solemn warning against judging the whole course of the world's events by such fleeting impressions. When one tries to base the idea of reincarnation upon fancies of this kind it merely acquires an evil reputation among all who would test it scientifically. For some decades attempts have been made in psychological literature to trace such passing impressions back to their origin. I myself once investigated such an impression. I had had an extraordinary vivid feeling that I had already been in a certain place. But I had certainly never been there during this present life. More exact investigation showed that at this place a smell was noticeable which had once been the accompaniment of an earlier vivid experience. The smell had brought with it a general feeling of remembrance, and there was nothing more. If psychoanalysis gave nothing else that was new, it at least called our attention to the vast unperceived realm from which waves are continually coming.

Recently people have got more clearly upon the track of certain characteristics which lie in their inherited qualities. If one examines the cases which are brought forward as examples of real remembrance, one finds oneself assailed by one doubt after another. In such cases people do not seem to know that the exact description of a place where one has never been is not the slightest proof that one must know it from a previous incarnation. People do not even come to the nearly related idea of a 'far sight'. They have no knowledge of a spiritual perception of people, things and places which they have not seen till then. If then one has learned from anthroposophy that there is such a thing as 'foresight', foresight of important events, towards which we are approaching, yes, even a foresight of the whole coming life itself, then one has reason enough for turning away from proofs like these.

And one grows still more circumspect at the sight of the spiritual trifling to which one is readily tempted by the idea of reincarnation. Who may I have been? What fate may I have already shared with this person? The danger is great that people may make their whole life so false by such a play of thought, that they can no longer act purely out of themselves. When those who are gifted as mediums join in the game and bring forward their fantastic imaginings about the connections between the different lives, we are not far from disaster. One may say candidly that if hostile powers wished to destroy people, they could lay hold of them at this point. So much vanity would come to meet them from human souls, so much desire for sensation, that the most evil distortions and corruptions would enter into the conduct of people's lives. When young people were trying to live in such imaginations, Rudolf Steiner sometimes said with emphasis: 'That would be pestilence.'

The earnest supporter of the idea of reincarnation must know all this; and not only know but say it himself, and not let his opponents be the first to say it. Much honest opposition to the idea of reincarnation comes from a knowledge of dangers of this kind or even from experience of their evil effects.

But does this mischief prove that the idea of reincarnation is an error? Have not the powers of destruction always used a truth to destroy truth? A spark of perception falls upon humanity: it can become a light, a light to the world, if people will tend it, but the will-o'-the-wisps lay hold of it in order to tempt people to the abyss. That has always been the tragedy of light upon earth. From the most brilliant discoveries of chemistry came chemical weapons. But does chemistry therefore lead people astray? Is it not the duty of humanity to wrest all truth from the powers of destruction?

And so we return to the question, are there such things as memories of a previous life? And it is certainly true that amid the many vague feelings, the many impure fancies, there are also quite other impressions, which must not be thrown overboard with them. For example, it occurs to some, when devoting themselves to the study of history, without thinking about themselves, 'I know this period from of old.' Perhaps there is nothing more than this, no personality with which they have been acquainted. They may allow this impression to rest. But at quite another place it occurs to them again. From the most different points of life they find this period indicated.

There are of course plenty of psychological explanations of this. And there is the latest phase of the psychology of heredity, with its investigations into memory. But they gradually notice that the impression has arisen out of a sphere quite different from that of the life of the soul, whose nature they have learned to know, with all that is impulsive and dreamy in it. They notice also that the impression is clearer, more spiritual, more informative; and that it is surrounded with a cloud of feelings of remembrance, which do not spring from their ordinary power of memory but rest somehow upon what is deeper in their personality. If they experience this, experience it again and again; if they learn to distinguish its peculiar qualities from those of the impressions which come out of other spheres; if they learn to observe the peculiar attitude to the world and the peculiar character of personality with which such impressions may appear, and if they come to experience them as breakings-through from another level of being, then they may ask themselves if they are not really on the track of a truth. In making these remarks we are not of course offering 'proofs' to convince doubters, but are giving a hint of experiences which must then be tested.

Finding the truth behind impressions

There is an infallible touchstone for such impressions. If they have the slightest thing to do with our vanity, they are false. Real memories, as Rudolf Steiner often said, are almost always connected with things of which we are ashamed. People have an uncanny capacity for avoiding such shame. Otherwise perhaps, these impressions would come more often into our consciousness. Only when all vanity, even the most concealed, is overcome or at least so well guarded against that no nebulous impressions can arise, then – and only then – can real truth emerge out of the depths. If our vanity leads us to find ourselves reflected in a famous person of the past, then the spirits of the depths would have succeeded in swindling us. In the book, *Rudolf Steiner Enters My Life,* I have offered the illuminating explanation which Rudolf Steiner gave of the fact that so many people lay claim to having been an important historical personage. As in this life one has a clearer picture of other people than one has of oneself, so it happens also when one looks back into the past. When we feel ourselves to have been related to some great person in the past, it need not be a mistake on our part, it need not be an illusion caused by our self-love, it is only that we were not that person ourselves, but perhaps one of those who revered him then.

The problem is this: how can we rid ourselves of all that proceeds from our turbid soul-life, and see clearly into the face of the facts? The turbidity is by no means *all* on the part of the brisk preachers of reincarnation. There is also a lack of clarity proceeding from the subconsciousness of their opponents. Many people admit freely that we have good reason to inquire thoroughly into our firmly settled habits of thinking, but they draw no logical conclusion from the admission. It is just in our unconscious thought about the relationship between body and soul that we have got into a materialistic rut. We push the action of the body upon the soul into the forefront of our interests in an unseemly way, and in spite of psychoanalysis very little attention is paid to the action of the soul upon the body. At most, one looks very closely at the sick and abnormal action – and this is especially true in psychoanalysis. But suspicion is a beneficial method of investigation only if it is applied impartially to all sides of the question.

Another source of many illusions is the common respect for words which one thinks mean something, but which merely conceal the problem. The word 'suggestion', for example, if it is not used in the technical sense, often plays a whimsical part in soothing us with the notion that we are thinking something.

But the chief opposition to the thought of reincarnation is at a deeper level. There are those who, quite understandably, dislike the idea of life after death if life on earth is uncomfortable. There is the whole trend of the spirit of the age, which turns to what is earthly, and fears that its powers in this life may be weakened by thoughts of a life beyond. And there is the effect made by pictures of the Christian heaven and hell (in which Lucifer's hand may be discerned), and of an easily-won blessedness which one would hesitate to forego. There is also the desire to be free of an existence of which one has had enough, if one judges all existence from the standpoint of materialism. These are some of the real points of opposition to the idea of reincarnation. And anyone who has once discovered them will look with just as much distrust upon what is advanced against the idea of reincarnation as upon what is brought forward in its favour.

The true scientific attitude towards the teaching of reincarnation is the following. Reincarnation can in no way be refuted by means of the scientific investigation of today. If anyone says or thinks the contrary, his contradiction cannot find ground of support, but is seated, if not in a resistance in his soul, then in habits of thought and feeling characteristic of this present age.

It is as clear as the sun that one cannot lay an idea like that of reincarnation upon the dissecting table; that neither the microscope nor the telescope can be so refined that it can bring reincarnation before human eyes. If one is to investigate its truth, methods of investigation must be found which can really reach this sphere. Anyone who asserts more than this, abandons the use of his reason and succumbs to prejudice, becomes 'unscientific'.

One may say, 'The teaching of reincarnation contains as presuppositions so many assertions about the relation of body to soul, of nature to spirit, of life to death, all of which I cannot test, that I cannot accept it.' Very well. But if instead of 'which I cannot test' one begins to say unconsciously 'which are unproven', one has set out upon the wrong path. Inadvertently one changes the true demand, that a truth must pass before the strict testing of the human mind, into the other demand, that a truth must be passed by the usual methods of investigation current today. One has every right to ask for a view of the world which denies none of the certain results of the painful, self-denying investigation of the last hundred years. But the request for a view of the world which must grow out of the usual means of thinking and investigating of today contains the presupposition that the experiences of the senses, and of intellectual thought, are the only means of perception which we have at our command. In this one is justified as far as the usual methods of proof used in abstract philosophical speculation and in religious speculation also are concerned, but not as regards the methods of perception employed in anthroposophical spiritual investigation. If people think they can say more in opposition to anthroposophy without studying its methods of investigation, they fall into serious scientific error.

The conviction of reincarnation

But the important question is, how does one become convinced of reincarnation? Do not all anthroposophists simply 'believe' in reincarnation not on the authority of the Bible, but only on Rudolf Steiner's authority?

The first thing to be said is that the number of people who have had experiences of reincarnation is much larger than is commonly thought. Such experiences cannot be waved aside by the verdict of materialism, because they actually break into the world of materialism in which one has lived.

As a historical witness let us at least mention Buddha. No one who has seen the clear inexorableness of his view of the world can take him to be a man of phantasy. And yet Buddha could say, 'In such a frame of mind, inward, purified, cleansed, virgin, cleared of dross, pliable, supple, steadfast, invulnerable, I directed my mind to the perceptions in my memory of earlier forms of existence. I remembered many earlier forms of existence, as it were one life, then two lives, then a hundred thousand lives. Then I remembered the many times when a world came into being, then the many times when a world crumbled to decay ... I was there, I had such and such a name, belonged to that family, that was my calling, such good and ill have I experienced, the end of my life was such ... Having died there, I entered again into existence. Thus I recalled to mind many different forms of existence.'

One must have great courage in one's own convictions if one would simply sweep away all discussion of this confession of one of the very greatest of human spirits. Yet – it can be no proof for us. And therefore let us also forego other historical testimonies, which take many forms and are often uncertain. Among the philosophical opinions the saying of the great sceptic, David Hume, is especially interesting, that metempsychosis, the transmigration of souls, is 'the only system of immortality to which philosophy can lend an ear'.

At present the number of people who tell us of impressions of reincarnation is increasing. Even if one takes only the twentieth part of these impressions seriously, there are still a sufficient number remaining to prevent our escaping from the subject, even with a large dose of scepticism; on the contrary, one acquires a scepticism about scepticism. One of the purest and most spiritual men whom I have known, told me that when he had bitter difficulties in his marriage, a picture arose in his soul, as he sought to find what was right. He saw a medieval cloister, and in it a monk who was giving his abbot trouble by his stubborn disobedience. He felt an inward connection with this picture. And with shame, he knew that it was his destiny now to make up for what he had done then. From that day on, his fate became easier for him.

We could tell of several similar accounts given by people who have had all the weight of present-day criticism directed at them, and whose experiences were anything but orgies of vanity. But, in order that we may avoid any appearance of wishing to use them to convince anyone, we shall not quote them. Let us say only that today what, during the last century and a half, kept darting in as an indistinct inkling is simply coming more clearly into people's consciousness. The professions of Lessing, Goethe and others are not the fossilised remains of past epochs (which may often enough exist) but the forerunners of human experiences to come.

Yet let us take up the question: how can we ourselves come to such experiences – or near to them? And with this question let us repeat the other: how is it that Rudolf Steiner has such confidence placed in him?

In the sphere of science of the spirit one is more fortunately placed than in the sphere of natural science. For the instrument of investigation is not an apparatus such as perhaps only an American university can afford, but the instrument of investigation is the human being. Even the person who never comes to having experiences of reincarnation of their own can by sound spiritual exercises collect such experiences of the relation of body to soul, of nature to spirit, that they can form a judgement whether a materialistic or a spiritual conception is the right one. They will not be content with an either/or. The more someone learns to meditate, the more the spiritual life appears before them in its own peculiar nature, its own individual laws, its own especial life; the more does nature become a curtain illuminated by the continually increasing light upon the stage behind; the more does the idea of further development, and also the idea of reincarnation, come within the illuminated circle of probability. We meet Lessing and Goethe again, when the spirit develops itself so strongly outwards and the 'I' so strongly from within that out of them a certainty of reincarnation comes. These are the real paths of man's future development which their genius foresaw.

Spiritual training for a sense of truth

By spiritual training people's whole attitude of mind is changed, and directed towards the spirit. Obviously, humanity is advancing towards such a spiritual development. The proof of this is the instinctive impulse which makes people today seek yoga or religious exercises, or methods of self-training. Mankind's most noble longings are directed towards the training and strengthening of the spirit, just because people feel that humanity, under the enormous pressure of outward life, will succumb to weakness and lassitude. At such moments it has always been mankind's fate to have many quacks and few physicians. But because so many people found that Rudolf Steiner gave answers to their questions they had otherwise sought in vain, and that he illuminated and explained their experiences that had begun to stir within themselves in an elementary way, he gathered round him a circle of educated and gifted people such as no other man of today has gathered. He has shown himself to be a great physician among many quacks.

These people have not by a long way had all the experiences which Rudolf Steiner had, or tested all the results which Rudolf Steiner obtained. But, because human beings are themselves the apparatus for a science of the spirit, it is possible to obtain from the experiences of their own soul, however primitive they may be in the spiritual sphere, a means of measuring what can be right and true in this sphere. Those who have gathered a few experiences through their own body will quickly be able to distinguish the physician from the quack. In this circle around Rudolf Steiner are many people who may perhaps seem to uphold dogmatically the teaching of reincarnation, but who yet have a personal right to speak on this subject because they are corroborated by dim experiences in their own soul. In this circle and wherever one is undertaking self-training in earnest there is an increasing number of impressions which lead in the direction of experiencing reincarnation. And the certainty increases that the universal advance of humanity is also towards the spirit, and that for the whole of humanity itself these impressions of reincarnation are becoming more abundant.

Only, until the number of those who are striving in the spirit becomes greater, one will always feel a kind of helplessness when meeting people who, through their clinging to the past, refuse to follow these new ways. And yet the truest views of the future may lie along roads where the ordinary point of view would set up the notice saying 'No entry'. An image can show with what certainty one may feel about it. A convinced land-lubber can never be brought to feel what people feel who can swim and trust themselves to water. The latter feel no less safe than the one who is on land, even when in swimming they no longer feel the ground under their feet. They do not deny that the man on the land must walk, and that the only movements which help him forward are the movements made in walking. But they refuse to believe the dogmatist about walking, if he lectures them from the land saying that the only movements which help people forwards are walking-movements.

And yet, spiritual training is not the only means which helps us forward. We have to admit that there is a primal sense of truth which, when supported by delicate impressions that scarcely enter into our consciousness and that we can nevertheless feel to be just, can lead to our taking up an attitude towards any particular view of the world. Problems are solved for us, which would otherwise have remained dark; explanations are brought to us which would otherwise have been denied to us; possibilities of life are opened to us which we can admit out of our deepest being and knowledge; powers are given to us for which we would otherwise have waited in vain, and yet it remains for us to make the ultimate verdict out of our inborn sense of truth. Without such certainties no one can live.

Anyone who thinks that this would open the floodgates to spiritual dilettantism and subjective caprice should remember that all the endeavours of those most skilled in forming theories of perception, have found no other criterion of truth but 'evidence'. And let anyone who asserts that the variety of the religious views of the world is a danger signal against such belief in evidence through one's primal sense of truth, study anthroposophical science of the spirit. It makes clear that no religion has ever been wrong, that only half-truths or truths suited to the age have been played off against one another in all religious conflicts, that a comprehensive view of the whole field is possible which puts every religion into its place in the history of the world and which lets us perceive, beyond the sphere of time, the concord of all religions. One will then recognise that this is no eclectic muddling together of the various colours in religious history, but that a higher perception has discovered the rainbow.

Rudolf Steiner often said that the ultimate truths require no external support from 'proofs' just as the starry heaven requires no scaffolding to support it. Just as the various constellations in the firmament bear and carry one another, so an ultimate view of the world may rest upon the mutual support of the highest truths. Whoever denies this is really waiting for external proofs based on sense-perceptible facts or on logical proofs. But in so doing they have given up their objectivity, they have opted for one view of the world, namely, for a materialistic and intellectual one. And even in that they rely more upon confidence than they realise, confidence in the general opinion, confidence in investigation, especially confidence that prejudgements have not entered into the representations and explanations of investigation, confidence in the academic authorities, and in much else.

The author's conviction

In face of the uncertainty which has come upon humanity because people have given up their primal sense of the truth in favour of an infallible tribunal of investigators, we must declare, however strange it may still sound to most ears, that there is a genuine possibility of living in communion with a real spiritual world, of moving freely and securely among higher realities, of feeling that one lives in the thought of divine wisdom in its essence.

Against the uncertainties which undoubtedly arise from this new point of view, we have only one means of defence, and no one can name another. It is a strict, unprejudiced spiritual attitude that seeks more and more to free itself from all subjective disturbances of the soul as well as from all recognised authorities; which accepts nothing which is not proved, but also rejects nothing without testing it; which takes the liberty and the right to think for itself, and to bring to bear upon any assertion its own sense of truth; which tests a truth by life, and life by a truth; which perceives in the attitude of resignation in the face of truth, only indolence, fear of life, and even spiritual peevishness; which has the courage to perceive even unaccustomed and awkward truths; which can remain long floating in suspense between 'yes' and 'no' without becoming dizzy; which, in a word, neither denies nor surrenders to any academy man's sense of truth, the right to the truth, or the courage to face the truth.

The author of this book confesses his belief in reincarnation on the following grounds. First, because on the ground of his own impressions, carefully tested a hundred times, he thinks he knows something about a life before birth. Secondly, because through years of free and severe spiritual exercises he has reached a conception of the relationship of body to soul which is in accordance not only with further development in a 'higher world' but also in accordance with reincarnation. And thirdly, because reincarnation has afforded the most satisfying solution to his quest, and the most illuminating fulfilment of his endeavours to find a satisfying view of the world.

He is convinced that the advance of humankind must

be made in this threefold way. The number of people will increase whose spiritual evolution and training will bring to them perceptions and experiences of the relation between body and soul, before which all materialism (conscious and unconscious) will break down, and will show the spirit acting upon bodies in such a way that the thought of reincarnation will approach nearer and nearer. The number of people will increase who will find in a view of the world which includes the thought of reincarnation the best satisfaction of their quest for answers to life's questions, the best explanation of their own life, the best fulfilment of their endeavours to find a view of the world.

Even if such people stop short in this question at the stage of probability, yet once a free attitude towards what is new is reached – an attitude that neither admits proofs where there are none, nor demands proof where there can be none, an attitude which is not tied to the past, but brings the greatest possible open-mindedness to the future; then let people's common search for truth prove whether we were right at present in upholding before western man the thought of reincarnation with a full sense of its real importance and of its meaning for life.

At present it is enough if the thought of reincarnation appears before the majority of people in such a form that they cannot refuse to admit in it a certain reasonableness, that they must grant it has more or less probability. All else will be contributed by the spiritual evolution of mankind itself. We are approaching a change in the general point of view, a reversal of the whole spiritual attitude. And for this we can wait.

Reincarnation in the Light of Religion

Nothing, almost nothing is said about reincarnation in the Bible. The idea that the individual human being is not on earth for the first time nor for the last time is certainly almost taken for granted in the older religions of mankind. But to the Bible, the religious guide of European humanity, it is foreign.

Indeed, when the teaching of reincarnation came up during the last century and received sympathetic hearing, traces of it were sought in the Bible. There was great activity, especially in English–American theosophical circles, in seeking Bible texts to support the new favourite theory. But only amateur dabblers could believe such proofs as were brought forward.

For example they pointed to the words in Psalm 90 (in some translations): 'You turn man to dust, and say, "Return, O children of man!"' Surely reincarnation is here clearly taught? Apart from the fact that no rabbi would ever have understood this passage like that, and therefore its secret intention of speaking of reincarnation would have failed in its effect – a more literal translation of the original text is: 'You turn people back to dust, saying, "Return to the dust, you mortals."' It is a return *into* the earth which is spoken of, not a return *on* to the earth. In the parallel measure of Hebrew poetry death is here spoken of, not rebirth. People are reminded that the God who has raised them up out of dust will bring them back to dust. There were also other explanations of this passage: 'You cause people to return to dust, saying, "Come again, you *other* mortals."' Even if this were correct, which is improbable, it would not say the least thing about reincarnation, but would rather speak against it.

Yet in the ninth chapter of John's gospel, in the passage where Christ meets the man born blind, there is the question, 'Rabbi, who sinned, this man or his parents, that he was born blind?' If it is declared to be possible that this man himself had sinned, because he had been born blind, then that must have happened in a previous life. So, is Christ here teaching about reincarnation? Certainly not. Here, of course, reincarnation appears in the background. We can well imagine that in the world of that time, when trade threw all kinds of people together, such ideas must have been discussed in the Holy Land also. It is also possible that out of the darkness of the mysteries it may have entered the minds of the disciples. It really was a significant moment in history when the disciples went to Christ and said, 'Master, a harsh fate here lies before us. Among people there are two entirely different explanations of such a fate. Israel teaches that the sins of the fathers are visited upon the children to the third and fourth generations. India teaches that men's misfortunes point to their own sins in an earlier incarnation. Which of these explanations is correct?' The disciples do not 'teach' reincarnation, but at most ask about it. Still less does Christ in this passage teach reincarnation. Rather he says, 'Neither this man nor his parents sinned, but this happened that the works of God might be displayed in him.'

So does Christ expressly reject reincarnation in this passage? If so, do we then not have here the biblical saying to prove the teaching of reincarnation to be false; or, to put it in a more modern and agreeable way, not in accordance with Christ's opinion but contradictory to it? But with that kind of approach we could prove almost anything – more than we would like. For one could argue that Christ also expressly rejected the Israelite point of view, that the sins of the fathers are visited on the children. Could he have done that? Could he have placed himself in opposition to the holiest Israelite possession – to the ten commandments – and not have brought upon himself the accusation of heresy? No. What Christ wished to tell the disciples can only be this. 'Your attitude to such a human misfortune is false. It is your task to look at what ought to come to pass.' The decisive question is not 'Why?' but 'To what end?' One can feel Christ's dislike of the dead way in which the disciples think, making a case of need into a problem for discussion, whilst Christ came to such a case in quite a different spirit, having perceived long before, through his will to help, what ought to happen. And so Christ's saying is an energetic rebuff to the merciless theorising with which such urgent need was often treated in the Holy Land as, for example, in the case of the women taken in adultery, immediately before (Jn 8:3–11).

For example, the Tamil proverb, 'If you want to see virtue and vice, then look at the sedan and those who carry it,' is conceived in a spirit as contradictory as possible to the spirit of Christ. And this will again become a danger when people busy themselves more earnestly with the thought of reincarnation. Then the spirit of Christ may rise up against people's unfeeling ways of thinking. But one cannot through such a saying of Christ overthrow an ancient human idea, without saying that one would be ready at the same time to break up the Old Testament.

John and Elijah

In a similar way we could discuss the pros and cons of other passages in the Bible. But there is one saying which we could not rightly treat in this way. It is one of Christ's own sayings, a part of the great declaration in which he placed his forerunner in the right light, when John had sent messengers from his prison to question Christ: 'And if you are willing to accept it, [John] is the Elijah who was to come. Whoever has ears let him hear.' (Mt 11:14f).

Again there is an especially important passage after the transfiguration.

> The disciples asked him, 'Why then do the teachers of the law say that Elijah must come first?' Jesus replied, 'To be sure, Elijah comes and will restore all things. But I tell you, Elijah has already come, and they did not recognise him, but have done to him everything they wished. In the same way the Son of Man is going to suffer at their hands.'
>
> Then the disciples understood that he was talking to them about John the Baptist. (Mt 17:10–13).

These are words which one ought to consider carefully. Certainly, if one has no other basis for the teaching of reincarnation, one could fall back on the explanation that *an* Elijah, a 'man in the spirit and power of Elijah', is meant. One could put beside it the announcement made by the angel to Zechariah (Lk 1:17): 'And he will go on before the Lord, in the spirit and power of Elijah.' One will perhaps point to the testimony of John himself, who answered the question, 'Are you Elijah?' by saying emphatically, 'I am not' (Jn 1:21). But can one prevent others from taking such a saying of Christ seriously, and understanding it literally? Even if John did not know about his former personality, that would be no proof that it had not existed. The Baptist's saying, 'I am not,' apart from the immediate meaning of the words, may stress the contrary of the 'I am' which from that time is constantly spoken by Christ in John's gospel. So that John – whether consciously or not – leads one away from his 'I' to the 'I' which now comes into the forefront. I, in my human personality, will be nothing but a voice calling for Christ, calling on behalf of Christ!

And if someone should reply, 'But even then it is an exceptional case that a man should return; and it is mentioned as an exceptional case in Christ's saying,' then one must answer again, 'But that proves that a man can come back. And who will say that this was, and has remained, an exceptional case? In the same passage it is suggested that it was possible for Jeremiah also to return. And in the Talmud, reincarnations are spoken of.'

It is only reluctantly that we enter into this game of question and answer. We are here speaking to people who can receive no new truth about human life without consulting the Bible. With them we must wrestle for the right to take a saying of Christ in its proper meaning. For the refusal to accept the thought of reincarnation has the upper hand in traditional Christianity today, and in all that, consciously or unconsciously, is influenced by it. But the path to reincarnation is nearer to the thought of the Bible than is usually supposed. Reasons, indeed, can be given why people's thoughts were at that time turned away from that path. This we shall still have to discuss.

The New Testament and reincarnation

At all events, on the other hand, it is noteworthy that in the New Testament there is nowhere to be found a saying which expressly refutes the thought of reincarnation in the great and wide sense in which we have explained it. The single saying which has been brought forward is not sufficient to deny it. That saying is found in the Epistle to the Hebrews (9:27f), 'Just as people are destined to die once, and after that to face judgement, so Christ was sacrificed once to take away the sins of many, and he will appear a second time, not to bear sin, but to bring salvation to those who are waiting for him.' From such a passage it can only be concluded that the teaching of reincarnation lay outside the apostle's circle of vision. His field of vision included the first and second coming of Christ. The contrast which stood before his soul is the distinction between the yearly sacrifice made by the high priest in the temple and the sacrifice of Christ made once only upon Golgotha. If Christ comes back, he comes again differently – just as a different life begins after death for a human being. To conclude from such a passage that this comparative sentence, 'as ... so', comes down against the teaching of reincarnation, reminds one of the bad old method of using scriptural proof. The only clear interpretation is that the author had no thought of the return of a human being to earth.

It is really certain that the teaching of reincarnation is not a scriptural teaching. There is not even a hint of it – apart from Christ's saying about John the Baptist. Anyone therefore who holds only to the teaching expressed in the Bible, must give up the idea of reincarnation.

But ought one still to take the field in such biblical armour against the perception of the truth? Once, when the Copernican idea of the universe arose in human thoughts, there was a struggle. Did the resistance to it, which was based on the Bible, help or hinder the Bible itself? And if anyone would say, 'That is something external, but now the question is an inward one; then it had to do with a view of the universe, but now with a view of life,' where is the dividing line? Is not this separating of outward from inward a helpless expedient, an impossibility? That was shown when the teaching of human evolution came. Is it external or inward? No, we do not honour the Bible if we make it a prison, neither for people nor for truth. We do not accept the Bible simply because it is the Bible, but because it is the truth. Therefore we accept the truth also, not because it is the Bible, but because it is the truth. If the last and highest truth is in the Bible, then we must seek the place of the spirit, from which this truth shines out beyond all other truths. We must not let this gift of highest truth become an injury to all other truths.

The resurrection

But how is it with the Christian proclamation of the resurrection? Quite apart from all individual sayings in the Bible, is it not as clear as the sun that the Christian idea of the resurrection can never be combined with any teaching of reincarnation whatsoever? And is not the resurrection the very heart of Christian hope for the future?

Against this, one might first point out what difficulties have increasingly grown up in human history concerning this very belief in the resurrection. The idea that the outworn physical body will be brought to life again, the idea that this will happen in a miraculous way, on one day for all people, and also the idea that in that day there will be a new earth similar to and yet quite other than our present earth – all these ideas come up against difficulties in our thinking consciousness which do not simply arise through malice, and which are increasingly hard to overcome. Even in the Middle Ages, the pious monks pondered much over questions in which the coming materialism already showed itself – what age were the people when they rose again, and what about those that had been burned? – and many questions like that. At present within Christianity there are two camps set against one another.

The one group appeals to the Bible, excludes all who doubt the unfathomable divine power, expects the intervention of God, which will surpass and put to shame all our thoughts of it, and without wishing to form any thoughts about life after death, yet hopes for the miraculous day of the resurrection of all. The other group is more cautious. In so far as they have not made the mistake of thinking that every individual soul is worthy of being preserved after death, they commit themselves more fully than the others to the divine wisdom, keeping an open mind and thinking that everything may be quite different from what we had imagined, and that a life which continues to evolve more highly after death may be at once our future, and the fulfilment of Christian hopes, and they are contented with every kind of immortality of the soul.

One can perceive that in these two directions the spirits of Judah and of Greece are living on within Christianity. These are the same opposites which fought fiercely together as Pharisee and Sadducee in the time of Christ. These are the same differences which we saw working themselves out nobly against one another, at the turn of the eighteenth to nineteenth century in Friedrich Gottlieb Klopstock and Friedrich Schleiermacher in the sphere of Christianity. Within the world of ideas which has existed up till now, they can never be at one. And so it remains only for the representatives of the one point of view to excommunicate the others from Christianity on account of their heathen ideas – and this is done with vehemence at the present day – and for the others who are calmer but weaker to look on the former party as late-born Jews, and to be conscious that they themselves represent a valid interest of today and even of Christianity itself.

This whole spiritual situation may be regarded as an indication that, as regards the fulfilment of Christian hopes, we have much to learn anew, or that perhaps we must look round for something quite different. Such a search for something quite different is to be found here and there in Christian literature. We remember the medieval story of the two monks from the same cloister who promised one another that the one who died first should appear the following night to the survivor and tell him what the world beyond was like. Because they had some doubts as to the possibility of an understanding between this world and the next, they agreed upon two words to be used in case of need: *taliter* – it is as we have imagined; *aliter* – it is different. After the death of one of them, his friend waited the following night for the message from the other side. And behold, the other did appear to him. But he said, *'totaliter aliter'* – it is totally different! In such tales there lives a deep awareness of the fundamental difference between the promise and the fulfilment. In the same way Charles Kingsley in his novel *Hypatia* makes the two women who have influenced the monk Philammon's life appear hand in hand to him as he is dying and say to him, 'That life after death is not such a one as you fancy; come, therefore, and behold with us what it is like.'

How does the teaching of reincarnation conceive of the resurrection? For it, the resurrection is divided into three experiences. We experience the first resurrection when we are permitted to begin a new life here upon earth. We live on upon the earth. But this continuing to live has nothing to do with what the Bible calls resurrection.

But now another fact enters our field of vision. People who have developed themselves higher and higher towards the spirit receive more and more the power of forming their body out of the spirit. They succeed more and more fully in finding out of their 'I', which becomes stronger and stronger, the bodily form which corresponds to their individuality, and to imprint this spirit-created bodily form on the physical embryo which inheritance has provided for them. This is the reason why some children resemble their parents less, and in others the inherited resemblance still prevails. Also for this reason, a more highly developed 'I' becomes ever more like itself in its successive incarnations.

And especially from Christ human beings receive such strong forces which act upon the body that the earthly body itself is increasingly compelled to yield and allow the 'spiritual body' to become more and more perfect. Yes, the special action of Christ, when people receive him living into themselves, is that he not only awakens those people inwardly in this life, that already in this life he gives them the experience of a new body which is evolving, but that he also gives this new body power to endure, and to be united with those individuals after this life is over. In coming times – and today the beginnings of them are here – there will always be a real resurrection when people who are united to Christ return to the earth. They will walk freely and ever more freely upon the earth. They have found *their* body – a spiritual body. In these aspects the fulfilment of the Christian hope of the resurrection already appears clearly, even if it proceeds through longer spaces of time than ordinary popular ideas have represented; more spiritually, and more ordered, does the Word become flesh in the sense of the spiritual principles in which the godhead works.

But even this is not the ultimate, is not the complete fulfilment. Rather a time will come when this earth really ends. It has then given to human beings all that it can give. From that time on it will fall into crumbling matter. But human beings who have become spiritual can now really live in the spirit. A purely spiritual form of existence will then be appropriate to human development. In it they are united with all those who have reached this earth's goal. A 'new earth' will become their homeland, not another star or celestial body, but an earth which has become spiritual. But only those who have found the inward union with 'the Lord who is the Spirit', with Christ in the great and broad sense perceived by spiritual investigation, will be united with Christ on this new earth. For others there follows not eternal damnation but a new period of grace, of such a kind that they live in a world suited to their will and their stage of development. There they receive judgement and grace from a higher world, but both of such a kind that new possibilities of ascent open up for them.

Here we can draw with only a few strokes the picture which is given of the future. One can well understand that to all those in whom the conceptions of established churches are still active, this picture will at first be strange and alienating, and perhaps even disillusioning. But on disimpassioned consideration they may realise that through it no essential Christian thought is lost, that everything only moves into much greater, broader perspective. Have we not long recognised that it is always thus with any 'fulfilment'? The mountain which we saw from a distance as one towering summit, as we draw near it appears as a mighty range with foothills and ranges, with valleys and ridges; and the final summit lies behind and above all.

Others who have lost the ideas held by the Christian churches will, however, see in such a description new possibilities of uniting themselves with Christian hope. On thinking it over they will recognise that not only is no essential Christian conception lost, but no essential knowledge of nature is contradicted. Only hasty conclusions, drawn from the point of view of natural science, are revealed and rejected. At last we are offered the opportunity of uniting meticulous thinking of today to the ancient hopes of humanity; within these hopes of humanity, of uniting the ancient sacred idea of reincarnation to Christianity's proclamation of the resurrection; of uniting them, not mechanically, but deeply organically, not eclectically, but in a higher perception whose unifying character is just as evident as its purifying character.

Paradise

But how about Christ's saying to the thief, 'Today you will be with me in paradise' (Lk 23:43), which has shone like a star of hope over so many a Christian deathbed? This very saying is difficult to reconcile with the usual picture of the resurrection. Is this being 'in paradise' a form of resurrection? Is it a rest before the resurrection? Is it an unconscious rest? How can Christ promise so confidently? Is it a conscious rest? Would not that be a 'life continuing after death'? What is the relation between the 'new earth' and the old 'paradise'? One must point clearly to such difficulties if one is to see the self-confidence of the 'Bible-believers' in its true light.

According to perceptions of anthroposophy, we must think in the following way about the fulfilment of such a saying. A person who is united to Christ will, from the moment of death, already feel the nearness of and fellowship with Christ much more strongly in the next higher world. As he leaves the physical form of existence, he is in 'paradise,' for this nearness to Christ is itself paradise; and this 'paradise' is itself a high sphere in which man can rise higher and higher. Even the lowest form of existence in this course of evolution may mean surpassing splendour, as compared with the form of life on earth. Nothing is missing from the fulfilment of such a saying, but it fits into the resurrection development as we have described it.

But if we think further of this concrete example, would it not be sobering and painful for the thief to discover that he had to descend again to earth, even if centuries later? And, on the other hand, would there not be far more really conscious Christians on the earth, if so many souls have really been in 'paradise'? By no means have as many people been 'in paradise' as have dreamt before their death that they would be. Many have perceived that they did not yet really belong to paradise. We can think of Selma Lagerlöf's legend,* in which Peter's mother, at the wish of her sorrowing son, was brought into paradise, but she was not at all suited for it. The thief also might after a time have longed for the earth again, because he had learned by then to see it quite differently and wished to do many things upon it better than he had done before. And are there not many people who bring with them to earth a kind of 'natural Christianity'? Are there not such people amongst free-thinkers, who do not recognise in established Christianity what they bear within themselves as secret knowledge, perhaps even as an essential substance within them? Many a person might be named who does not belong to Christianity in his external life, only because he surmises there is a greater Christianity than that which meets him here. Are there not also such men among far-off peoples? Rabindranath Tagore? Gandhi? What someone has really acquired of essential Christianity – not of Christian thought – will remain theirs. But perhaps this is less than most 'Christians' think they have. Perhaps we ourselves if we had to guide the universe according to our own estimate, would send most 'Christians' back to earth.

Here also we find that a rethinking about this is necessary, and that in this rethinking no essential Christian truth is lost, that the Christian view of the world gains in sober earnestness and moral greatness. Such a Christianity grows, not only in intellectual probability, but also in lifelike reality.

---

* Selma Lagerlöf, 'Our Lord and Saint Peter' in *Christ Legends*.

Biblical sayings

Further, for the first time, it becomes possible to think clearly about some of the sayings in the Bible. For example, the saying, 'everyone will have to give account on the day of judgement for every empty word they have spoken' (Mt 12:36). What fulfilment can we think of for such a saying? Because it is impossible for us to think of a court of judgement in which every hasty word will be discussed, we form no idea, and so this saying disappears from our vision, and is no longer taken seriously. Does not such a saying call for another method of forming ideas, in which the inaccessibility of the picture is overcome and yet its penetrating power is preserved?

After death, as spiritual investigation recognises, a man will live back again his whole life in a more spiritual form of being. This is the 'second judgement' which awaits him after he has looked at the picture of his life as it arises out of his etheric body. It is not yet the last. As he now goes backwards he comes to all the places where he has spread useless talk around him. He becomes sensitive to the want of harmony between this chatter and the depths of the world's reality, and is shocked by it. Not 'in a sense', but actually, he stands before the tribunal of the spiritual world. Along with him the eyes of higher beings are looking into his life. Over him is the cosmic judgement out of the higher worlds, bringing before his remembrance every single word. In him awakes a feeling of responsibility for all that he has sent into the world. The earthly experience of judgement which we have before us in the picture of Christ gives is itself only a defective image of the last judgement towards which we are all going, which is the nature of the world itself.

Hans von Bülow, the famous nineteenth-century musician, is said to have been shocked when he heard for the first time a recording of a Beethoven sonata which he himself had played. He would not believe that it was he who had played it. In the inexorable objectivity of the machine for perhaps the first time he became aware of the difference between what he had wished and had also inwardly heard, and that part of it to which he had given expression. It was a little last judgement, pronounced by a discordant voice. The phonograph recording had already brought some of the freer Protestant theologians to similar allusions to the nature of the last judgement, saying in a sermon: 'What you say, you are speaking into a great phonograph, and at the last day it will sound back to you again.' Such comparisons are unspiritual and materialistically coarse in comparison with the overwhelmingly real spiritual nature of the actual facts. But do not external images of higher realities thrust themselves into many modern discoveries?

'Truly I tell you, whatever you did for one of the least of these brothers and sisters of mine, you did for me' (Mt 25:40). Such a saying will not be fulfilled by some external voice speaking audibly sometime, somewhere, directing itself to us above all others, so that we accept its judgement upon its own authority; but it will be fulfilled when Christ's voice becomes clearly heard by us in the world above this one. We enter then into a new world in which we no longer shut ourselves off, in which we can no longer deceive, in which we appear in the cosmic connection as those persons whom we really are. In that inescapable court of justice we hear the divine voice. We recognise it to be the same voice which spoke to us on earth through Christ. We recognise that evolution towards what is divine, which we ought to have served, in the people whom we meet. We recognise in ourselves the real being which perhaps our outward confession has completely contradicted. How literal and how gravely serious a fulfilment may this saying then have: 'I never knew you. Away from me, you evildoers' (Mt 7:23).

But the other saying also becomes true: 'whoever hears my word and believes him who sent me has eternal life and will not be judged but has crossed over from death to life' (Jn 5:24).

The first two millennia of Christianity

If all this is true, why have people not been aware of it before? Why does the Bible itself not express or even hint at such a method of fulfilment? We shall not look at the traces of the thought of reincarnation that are still found in the most ancient Christian writings, especially among the Gnostics and Manicheans. Only too readily do the circles of theosophists, who believe in reincarnation, point to all the great minds in history, among them not only the Church fathers, Origen and Clement of Alexandria, but also to Gregory of Nyssa, Philo, Jerome, even to Justin Martyr and Tertullian. In fact many of these the idea spoke of future development in other worlds, but seldom or never expressed the opinion that there is a return to this earth. And yet this question requires thorough investigation. Till now, Christian theology has brought only lukewarm interest to it. To us the more pertinent question is: does anthroposophical investigation have anything illuminating to say about why Christianity, up until now, has kept the thought of reincarnation so remote?

Anthroposophy gives the following answer. In the great path of human destiny it was preordained that for two thousand years humanity should completely lose the idea of reincarnation. It was the time during which the earth was to be mastered by humanity. The perspective was, as it were, obscured by clouds, and people's gaze was directed entirely down towards the earth. They had to dig deep here, and could do this the more undisturbed, if the view before him was undazzled from higher realms.

Two thousand years is the period of time during which everyone normally passes through two incarnations, one male, and one female, which contain totally different experiences. In these two millennia human beings saw their life, not once but twice, enclosed between birth and death, so that they might discover all that is to be seen between them. People would never have taken the earth as seriously – the east proves this – as they ought to take it; they would never have studied their earthly home with such interest, would never have gained an earthly 'I' in its solidity, if their gaze had always been directed to the cosmic picture around the earth. In history humanity always receives one gift after another, one gift at the cost of another. We should not have had all the culture of the individual as it exists in the west if we had retained the idea of reincarnation, if we had not resolutely turned towards the earth, and the divine powers had not arranged for this turning. But now we can win back this thought of reincarnation, yet in a form in which the physical earth with all its riches, and the individual life with all its importance, and the personal 'I' with all its value, can have their full rights.

To this we may add that as it were Christ had to be received by humanity out of the densest form of earthly existence. As we look at the successive millennia, we find that Christ appeared on earth just at the point of time when humanity set out on its journey through the valley of the earth. It is therefore not without divine significance that Jesus was baptised at the deepest point in the surface of the earth. For the earth itself is not merely a lump of matter. From the deepest depths, humanity had to enter into Christ's life. From the very bottom of earthly need, not only with their sins but also with their remoteness from the spirit, people had to receive the new meaning of the earth. Christ entered matter at its very densest, which was shaping the human body and ultimately bringing about its destruction. Only through this is it possible for humanity now to ascend, through and with Christ.

These thoughts can be rejected as a superfluous and ingenious apology for the inconvenient fact that nothing about reincarnation can be found in the Bible, or perhaps, by their inward intrinsic truth and their illumination of the historical picture, they give a possible explanation of spiritual things which moves upon a higher plane.

Protestant theology on reincarnation

The spiritual vision of Rudolf Steiner revealed that Christ himself did not wish that in the first period of Christianity reincarnation should be spoken about, but that in the present day this truth should gradually dawn upon humanity. Such an insight can be tested against present-day Protestant theology which is stirring itself. (Catholic theology is a much less adequate expression of the deeper movements of the time, through its imprisonment in dogma.) To quote Otto Pfleiderer: 'The Protestant doctrine of the eternal stability of the two different conditions of departed souls must be remodelled into the thought of an endless multiplicity of forms and stages of development in the life beyond, in which there is room for infinite love to exercise continually its edifying wisdom.' That is not reincarnation, but it is on the way to the truth of it. We must mention also Ernst Troeltsch's saying: 'It may be predestination, or it may be reincarnation which reveals the secret – we do not know.' And still one more saying may be quoted which is uttered by a theologian who is not one of the best known, but which is yet not without interest as a historical judgement. Speaking of the rejection of purgatory by the reformers, Ernst Bruhn says, 'Because of the thicket of barren superstition, they did not see the sleeping problem.'

But in general Protestant theology remains silent as the grave, even where it does not share that concentration upon the past as in the work of Karl Barth and his school. If one opens the big encyclopaedias and looks under 'reincarnation' or 'transmigration of souls' there is deep silence, or perhaps some laborious historical study, scarcely a refutation. And through refutation recognition begins. Even the controversial writings against anthroposophy contain at most a few reckless assertions, which because of their wretchedness convince no one who takes the problem seriously. Or there are the free ethical studies of the moral wickedness of the teaching of reincarnation, which again show no acquaintance with the real facts.

A Protestant refutation

In Protestant literature I know of only one single pertinent refutation of the teaching of reincarnation. I shall cite it verbally and deal with it seriously.

In the first place, our insight into the connection between body and soul and our insight into the immeasurable difference between individuals has become so lively and strong that we are obliged to say: 'My soul is suited to no other body than to my own; in every other body it must of necessity become something different.' Aristotle already declared in opposition to Pythagoras that to assert that one soul could pass through very different bodies is to assert that a carpenter can do his work with a flute just as well as with an axe. And even if one calls what passes from one body to another, not soul but karma, or some thing of the sort, yet as it

lives in another body it is no longer that which it
has been, is really not that which evolution requires,
namely my fully personal 'I'. Our body is not so
much a matter of chance, is not so exchangeable
as the doctrine of reincarnation presupposes. One
would be obliged in that case to assert that it is the
soul alone which freely creates its bodies according
to its previous behaviour – an assertion which
scarcely anyone can maintain in the face of the facts
about the origin of man and animal.

The author is quite right if it were the same soul which
had to live in the new body. But this is not so. According to
anthroposophical investigation, the soul spends a period of
some centuries in the higher world before it gets ready for an
earthly life again. It works out all that it has learned in the
past life, and under the guidance of divine powers it unfolds
out of these experiences the plan for a new life. But by then it
becomes different and requires another body. It can no longer
use its former body.

But when at the end of the passage quoted the natural origin
of man is pointed to, by way of objection, then we have in the
anthroposophical teaching of reincarnation a form of this
idea which takes full cognisance of all the facts of heredity.
We have already discussed this thoroughly. Let anyone who
holds it to be a myth that the soul works unconsciously upon
the body, think how even a climate works upon a living entity
adapting the body. A soul, certainly, is not a 'fully personal
"I"' when it thus works creatively on the body. But, how often
are we *not* that, during our own lives? How little, even, are
we that?

The second objection of our author is concerned with
memory.

In addition to this, the idea of evolution, of becoming perfect, on which this is based, must appear to us to be unsatisfying. Once we have become conscious beings, living personalities, there is only one idea of evolution which is worthy of humanity and ethically satisfying, namely, that we should gather living experiences, and that upon the ground of these experiences, which we gradually come to understand better and to explain more correctly as we compare them with new experiences and thus enrich them, we should deliberately advance towards the goal of goodness. Into this advance towards ethical perfection the teaching of the transmigration of souls brings something ghostlike. My experiences are extinguished, as far as they are valuable, namely, as experiences of my conscious 'I', and accompany me like a kind of natural fate, into a new existence, as a dark force of nature to which I have formerly succumbed, without retaining the free relationship to them of my will. Experiences are a much too living and movable possession to bear that sort of petrification, which the doctrine of reincarnation presupposes. In this way, perhaps, an embryo may be evolved but never an ethical being. Although such ideas may have been held in India, where they have still little understanding of the finer values of personality, among us it is no longer possible to maintain such a conception.

Here again, anything which is illuminating in this argument disappears as soon as one looks more closely at it. Does a psychology which says that we evolve only by means of our conscious experiences really correspond with the facts of life?

It is often those impressions which do not enter fully into our consciousness which have the strongest effect upon us: for example, our first youthful impressions, the impressions of powerful experiences which we do not expressly think about afterwards, the impressions of our dreams, which enter only occasionally into the light of consciousness. Such experiences are not ghostly, but matters of feeling. One cannot call them petrifactions; they are the seeds of life. Everyone who has kept a diary for a number of years will know how surprised we are when we stray about among old memories, and ask ourselves time and again, 'What! Did I ever think that? Did I intend to do that? How different life would have been if I had held fast to these perceptions, to these intentions.' If this is true of this one life, and in the course of a few years of consciousness, would it not be still more true of experiences which we have had in an earlier existence, in other conditions of soul, in quite different bodies? No, the simplest experiences in life, the simplest perceptions in the soul, contradict such declarations of psychology.

Conscious development is certainly the ideal. In the far future it will become a reality. Then our experiences of earlier earthly lives will also come clearly to light, and become a part of our will to ascend. But in the present stage of human development this desire can have only very limited fulfilment.

> And lastly, the idea of justice which lies at the bottom of this idea of reincarnation is unacceptable to us. Herder already pointed this out in his polemic against Lessing, when he said, 'The hidden tiger in the human race is now a real tiger, without obligations, without conscience, yet these often trouble him. Now he makes a rush and mangles his prey with hunger, thirst and appetite, urged on by inward desire, which he only now satisfies entirely. That was the wish of the human tiger, that was his

will. Instead of being punished he is rewarded.
He is that which he willed to be, and which once in
his human form, he was very imperfectly!' To this we
add that the higher conceptions of justice demand
that he who is condemned and punished must be
in a position to see that the punishment is just, and
to transform it voluntarily into atonement. Where
the possibility of this insight is lacking, as in small
children or the mentally disordered, then, according
to our ideas the punishment is ethically unjust. We
think more highly of the ethical constitution of this
world than to think of it as a kind of bank where
possessions are paid out to heirs, who do not know
very well how they came to get them. Yet the doctrine
of reincarnation ultimately teaches that there is a
kind of mechanical reckoning made with human life,
but there is no real justice or training of spirits.

We do not need to point out that here the author, along with
Herder, is combating a form of the teaching of reincarnation
with which anthroposophical perception has nothing to
do. Man remains man, and never again becomes an animal.
People of past centuries have indeed had all kinds of visions
of animals when they perceived clairvoyantly the astral body
of the dead. Anthroposophy teaches that in man every kind of
animal being, according to the nature of its soul, is summed
up, and tamed into humanity; that one can perceive in the
human astral body this property of the animal soul, which is
the basis of the visible animals as well as of man. The heraldic
animals in the coats of arms of ancient families may have been
designed out of such a perception. But it is a misunderstanding,
arising from a false and degenerate form of the teaching of
reincarnation, to draw from such impressions the conclusion
that a man actually lives as an animal after a later birth.

So now there remains only the question of justice. But does not even a wise training of children consist in bringing them into a new situation after they have fully tried out what they have experienced earlier, so that one may see what they have learned from their experiences, without for ever explaining to them the art of education? It is not a question of 'punishment', nor of 'expiation'; these are pre-Christian ideas from which one is here drawing conclusions, as they are drawn in modern inflictions of punishment. It is a question of a hidden but no less real and active training. The tiger in human form does not become a real tiger who may tear and mangle to his heart's content, but he becomes a human being faced by a tiger in human form, and who now experiences the action of the tiger nature upon his own body, and who enriches his experiences by acquiring something he has not yet held. What is of far greater importance is what happens, and not the mere knowing.

A holy justice reigns in destiny, leading people rightly as a child is led, even when they do not yet understand it at all. She allows them gradually, according to their ripening understanding, to share her own wisdom. If today we do not see the use of a particular destiny, is that a proof that we shall not see it in the future? Do we not, even in this life, need to grow ripe for the blessing that comes from a misfortune, before we receive the blessing? And is it not possible that humanity has now, and only now, reached the stage when it steps out of childhood into riper years, and so is only now learning something of the deeper wisdom of destiny?

We have now dispassionately tested the objections of this Protestant theologian without considering his personality, but we owe it to the reader to mention his name. I myself am the author, in an essay which I published in the *Süddeutsche Monatshefte,* May 1910. It was a dispensation of destiny that I should bring together all the evidence against the teaching of reincarnation, so that then – from the beginning of 1911 – I should make the acquaintance of a teaching of reincarnation which these arguments did not touch.

Yet even then in dealing only critically with the teaching of reincarnation, I tried through it to show that the present-day Protestant's idea of life after death is inadequate, and that, at least speculatively – I could not then see it otherwise – some opinions expressed within the teaching of reincarnation could also find their place within Christianity.

> Without doubt, in the teaching of the transmigration of souls, some truths are admitted to be valid, which are too briefly treated in traditional church doctrine. In respect of the life after death, traditional church teaching knows only heaven and hell. But it is a fact of experience, to which we cannot shut our eyes, that no one dies who would not be too good for hell and too bad for heaven. And so, within the Catholic Church the teaching of purgatory has come into existence as the doctrine of an intermediate state, although there was no sufficient basis for it in the Bible. The Reformers refused to accept the idea of purgatory, because they wished to hold entirely by the Bible, and feared the notorious misuse of this teaching ...
>
> Everyone is free to accept or reject a belief in a life beyond: those, however, who wish to hold fast to such a belief, and who ponder things in the light of it, come to these conclusions, if their ethical feeling is highly developed. First, man's destiny must not be regarded as being uniform, but is quite differently shaped in each individual case. Secondly, there cannot be simply a complete break between this life and the life to come, but there

must be an inner connection, which is exact even in its details. Thirdly, there can be no question of a magical transformation, but there must be a further development of that which was begun in this life.

These three statements, can be united with the very kernel of the biblical ideas, and cannot be rejected by anyone who accepts Bismarck's saying: 'That death is *an* end, I see indeed, but that it is *the* end, I can never believe.' The truth in the doctrine of the transmigration of souls is that it gives living expression to these three thoughts. Upon this depends its power to attract so many of those who will not give up a belief in the life beyond.

In this passage I look forward to ideas of the life beyond in which the truths of reincarnation is united to the religious and ethical truths revealed in Christianity.

Reincarnation and the essence of Christianity

The author of this book feels himself to be so inwardly united with Christianity that the idea of reincarnation – in spite of all that which can be said for it – would be inessential and unimportant, if he had not gradually come to perceive how organically it is bound up with the deepest Christian impulse. In the book *Rudolf Steiner Enters my Life,* I wrote as follows upon this subject.

> Karma and reincarnation – the laws of destiny and rebirth. It is said they are exactly contrary to the Christian experience of grace and the biblical gospel of salvation. Over against this let it be stated with all emphasis that in our time both these truths,

although they are not found in the Bible, can be recognised as Christian truths. For me they are not so much scientific results of spiritual research with which Christianity has to come to terms – although they are that too – but far rather actual demands of Christianity when it is rightly understood.

Think of it for a moment: someone passes into the higher world. How will it be with them? For a time they may rejoice to find themselves free of the earth and all its misery. But then, if they are allowed a prayer – what will it be? They will surely wish again to meet all those human beings whom they wronged in earthly life, and will crave for the opportunity to do good to those whom they wronged on earth. 'Grace' will lie precisely in this, that they ask if this may be granted. The law of karma may have appeared in the east as irrevocable world-necessity – in the light of Christ it becomes an act of grace, our own free wish. But *that* act of grace – the only one of which we usually hear mention – namely that a person has been seized by the reality of Christ, *that* act of grace must have gone before in order to make such a wish possible at all.

And suppose the person in the other world is allowed a second request – what will they wish? They will wish that they may help the Christ where his task is heaviest and most menaced, where Christ himself suffers and has to fight most bitterly. This wish, if it were fulfilled, would lead the person back again to the earth.

It is *not* Christian to long for rest and blessedness far from the miseries of earth. It *is* Christian to bear within one the consciousness which once brought Christ from heaven to earth, to find one's joy in

> being like him and to work with him, wherever
> he may need us. The whole truth of the Christian
> doctrine of resurrection remains intact and – as
> could be shown in a theological treatise – indeed
> increases in clarity and grandeur.*

Even in these thoughts it is not intended to give an external proof of reincarnation. Only we must grapple with the opinion which, in discussions about reincarnation, expresses itself in the following words: 'But I do not want to be reincarnated!' It is out of this corner of the will that the real resistance to the teaching of reincarnation proceeds. If it is once seen that such an opinion is not the only possible Christian opinion, that it is not even a Christian opinion at all, then the field is free from impure moods and struggles. Then a calm objective pronouncement can be given. Let everyone who confesses himself to be a Christian put to himself this question today when the idea of reincarnation comes up: 'Would you be prepared to recognise and accept the world to be such as it appears to be from the thought of reincarnation? Would you be ready to think of death, judgement and the perfecting of the soul, and could you bear them as they appear to be through the teaching of reincarnation? Would you, above all, be willing to allow yourself to be sent back to earth, if it were the divine will, if it should be necessary for the work of Christ?' If you can answer yes to those questions, then one may hope to reach a pure decision. Otherwise, religion might again become the opponent of the truth, as happened on similar grounds in the case of Copernicus. Only in a spirit freed from evil growths can new truths arise in such a way that their true life force is revealed.

* *Rudolf Steiner Enters my Life,* pp. 125f.

And here we are not dealing with any new thought in particular, but with a new way of looking at the world, which suggests and brings to us a broader, more serious, purer, more heroic, greater Christianity. In this view of the world we must not think that after death we are free of all the odds and ends of earthly life, and leave all else, whether development or transformation, to the divine will, with only one reservation, namely, that we have no more to do with the earth. On the contrary, after death we find fulfilment of what has been prepared in us, but we find also earnest slow development, and above all we remain united with our earthly home, more deeply and enduringly than we had formerly thought. We must not think of the earth as being only a place of sin and need, worthy of destruction when it has served as a training-school for humanity, but that the earth is capable of evolution, that it has still to endure a long time, giving to us and expecting from us; that it is and remains the place of humanity, woven far beyond the single life into the destiny of all men. We must not think that Christ once touched this earth and since then looks down upon it from a higher world, but that he has united himself lastingly with the earth and carries on his work upon earth, in those who have entered into close connection with him, towards a goal which consists not in the saving of individual men, but in a new earth and a new humanity.

The question is not, 'What does the Bible say about reincarnation?' but much more, 'What does the innermost mind of Christ say about reincarnation? Which view of the growth of the world unites us more deeply with Christ's will, which is directed not merely from earth to heaven, but also from heaven to earth?'

Rudolf Steiner has often compared the emergence of the truth of reincarnation with the discovery by Copernicus of the laws of the starry heavens. Then our idea of space was shattered, now time. Then Christianity had to find its way into a greater world, now into a greater timespan. In both cases the knowledge came from outside the Church. Christianity will not find its death in such knowledge, but its resurrection. One can already clearly see that through such new knowledge, Christianity will be placed in a position to fulfil better the three demands made upon it at the present day: namely, to acquire a new understanding of the real knowledge gained in a scientific age; to acquire a new understanding of the earth and its tasks, including social questions; to acquire a new understanding of the different religions of the earth, their meaning for history and their hidden truths.

Reincarnation in the Light of Ethics

One often hears from opponents of the idea of reincarnation that the idea does serious harm to ethical life. People defer serious effort because they still have time and no longer feel the full weight of obligation in this life. They feel themselves powerless under an inescapable law, their fate predestined in this life and also fettered in a future life. A calculating morality, instead of a living in freedom, enters into their life. As evidence of such assertions, tales of missionaries are brought forward, of how in the east under the rule of the law of karma life is without hope.

Missionaries may be admirable men, yet one would not place into their hands the final decision as to the value of religions. Nor does the India of today tell us much about the India of former days, and a degenerate teaching of the transmigration of souls tells us little about a future knowledge of reincarnation which is illuminated by Christianity.

Always, when a new view was brought forward, the ruin of humanity was prophesied. And those who prophesied have seldom been real prophets. When Luther came announcing the grace of God, Catholic theologians painted in dark colours the coming immorality. Since then the centuries have pronounced judgement, and the morality of Protestant regions can hold up its head before the morality of Catholic regions. Then the Lutherans seized their palettes and sought the darkest colours when they heard of Calvin's doctrine of election (that God chooses a particular person for a particular task or relationship like eternal life, in other words predestination). The world was to go under in swathes of hopelessness and despair. The truth was otherwise. In Protestant regions that held this doctrine of election, a new morality unfolded itself. Will people never learn from such experiences? Will people never allow those to speak who have for years led their lives in the light of the idea of reincarnation? Will people again of themselves decide what must be the effect of an opinion, without seeing what effect it actually has?

Let us start from personal experience. I have often had to do with people who laid bare their fate to me. They were seeking to understand what had happened to them. Old Christian thought had no place in their souls. In general, neither it nor what Church opinion has to say about human destiny held them any longer. Should I? Should I not? Sometimes I deliberated a long time whether I could undertake the responsibility of introducing thoughts of reincarnation into someone's life, whether I myself were sure enough of its truth. Ultimately – some ten or twenty years ago – I said something like this: 'How would it be if you were to consider whether your present fate is connected with events and acts of your past life? Might not some destiny derived from a past life be now seeking its equalisation?'

'What, do you believe that we have already been upon the earth?'

'What I believe does not matter. We shall try together to seek for a light upon the present case. Earnest men have held reincarnation to be possible, even certain. Under such a presupposition how should we have to think about life?'

When I think today about the many hours in which I have thought about destiny in a similar way along with other people – never dogmatically, always hypothetically; never fancifully, always ethically – there remains clearly in my remembrance how gently the gates opened to a higher understanding of destiny, to a higher surmise of it. Comfort came down, comfort such as flows from a living surmise of a wise governance, of whose secrets people can catch many a glimmering if they calmly review their own past life. The way to understanding was opened; and they felt themselves to be taken seriously as people of today, because their wish to understand was not discouraged but sustained and carefully guided.

I know well what objections may be raised. People who are inclined to ethically religious views will say, 'One ought not in studying destiny to ask "Why?" but ought to try to solve the problem by asking, "To what end?" The question "Why?" leads to uncertainty; the question "To what end?" leads along a definite path and shows us at least the first steps out of our need. And the question "Why?" is illuminated only when the question "To what end?" is answered.' Certainly, one may talk thus. For years I myself did not know any other answer. And in many cases it will be the right answer. But some special case may reveal to one that in such an answer a deep resignation speaks, that through such an answer a living need, especially of today, may be merely repressed.

A mother has a child with an incurable mental handicap. What can one say to her? The best that can be said from a conventional religious point of view is in the following. If there were no destinies which were completely dark and hopeless, people could not develop the deepest trust in the divine guidance of their life. Those impressions of life by which they receives light from above ought to strengthen them for those in which at first only darkness surrounds them. People are tested and tried thus, and their union with God becomes perfect and unconditional. And again, unless there were those who could never thank us for what we did for them, because their minds were completely darkened, then our love for others could not attain to the purest unselfishness, to perfect greatness.

One can speak warmly and effectively about that, and the best pastors in the past spoke like that. But does one not feel the inhumanity which infects such consolation? Out of her love the mother will put the agonised question, 'But what will become of my child? Is it right and just that my child suffer this fate so that I may learn, so that I may be proved? How can anyone or any god permit a human being to become the means to an end for another person's sake?' To this the pastor can only say, 'We shall try to illuminate this dark destiny from the point where we ourselves stand, by the effect which it has upon ourselves. And starting from this, we shall try to find the conviction that will also throw light on the point where we do not stand.' But if the pastor has a heart, he will not let all paths end so incomprehensibly, but will feel compelled at least to light a tiny candle of hope, with some kind of 'perhaps'.

When I was in such a situation, I learned one day that Rudolf Steiner's investigations had shown that highly gifted philanthropists have sometimes had mental handicaps in earlier lives and were thrown completely upon the loving help of those around them. This loving help may have penetrated directly into their heart and mind without being intercepted and analysed by their understanding. The experiences of such a life might indeed be changed into a deep, instinctive love of humanity.

I cannot describe the impression this report made upon me. I now became conscious how much one had sought inwardly for such solutions or possibilities of a solution; how much one had hoped to receive them from a higher world after death. It passed over my soul like a mighty foretaste of the revelations which await us after death. Certainly we have to take great care with such information – with our grimy hands we can soil everything, and we have soiled everything that has been given us. But when afterwards, in talking with a mother, the curtain which hid these possibilities was carefully raised, then I knew why such a sight has been given today.

Individual destiny

What earlier generations said about sorrow does not lose its value. For 'trust' also there remains a wide field; indeed a new realm is opened to it. But a new friend enters human life – one who appeals to people of today. People of today share in the events of the world more freely and more consciously, and also live their own life more freely and consciously. It is not caused by insolence and impertinence, but by an awakened power of thinking and a strengthened consciousness of freedom. The most superficial person may say, 'How have I deserved this?' But this question may also be asked by an 'I' striving to become one with a greater 'I', by an 'I' feeling in its destiny that it can become one with this greater 'I' only if it has found in it a deep morality, by an 'I' that shapes its own destiny from its insight into such a higher 'I'.

But have we now solved the question of destiny? Is it not merely pushed further away? How did it come about that in earlier lives people had to bear differing fates, possessed differing faculties, had to stand differing trials? Experience teaches that people do not feel the need of questioning further and further back, to the extent that might be theoretically conceived. It is enough for people to see some distance along the path, both backwards and forwards, and from this stretch to divine the whole. Plenty of secrets remain. Nothing is more childish than to reproach people of discernment with destroying 'secrecy'. The world around us has such a wealth of secrets that we might go on 'destroying' calmly for some millions of years, and then, still questioning, stand before the primal secret. It is just as naive to tell them they have only pushed the problem further away. In the realm of physics one is thankful to anyone who can push the problem only a little way further off, and one expects no more than that from one human life. But through the knowledge of reincarnation, a highly significant step forward has been taken in solving the question of human life and destiny.

The dramas of Ibsen show how modern humanity has reached this question. And the teaching of heredity has immensely increased the burden of it. Humanity will break down, not under the weight of the teaching of reincarnation, but under the weight of the teaching of heredity, unless the teaching of reincarnation is added to it. The thought of heredity drives human beings to suicide, the thought of reincarnation leads them to resurrection. It gives them a new power of saying 'Yes' to their destiny, and a new power of saying 'No' to it. Yes, because they understand it; no, because they see the possibility of release. Rudolf Steiner has shown how in many kinds of diseases the effects of perversity of soul in a former life continue to act, and how, also, in these diseases the bodily condition gives help against an existing lack of character.

Human beings of the future will be able to carry on the struggle with their destiny in a grander style. They will see their destiny to be greater than life. They will be able to lift their head above the clouds which hem in their fate. Out of a higher 'I', they will be able to fit this one life into the greater plan for life. They will redemptively endure a heavy fate right to its end and lift the meaning of this fate upon a higher path across the ages. It will no longer be kismet which they endure, that is the 'share' of destiny allotted to them, no longer fate, that is God's predestined decree which is fulfilled in them. Rather they will talk with their angel, and as they speak with their angel it is the higher 'I' speaking within them. And as they say 'Yes' to destiny, their higher 'I' enters and takes up its lasting abode with them. All people feel the hand of kismet, many feel the hand of fate. Few look into the face of destiny and see in it the face of the divine spirit, which welds the little destinies of life into a great whole above time and space. Sometimes, indeed, when we survey our destiny with purer and freer gaze, we feel that we would ourselves have disciplined ourselves in no other way.

At such moments we are looking at our lives through the eyes of our angel. We are helped to take this view of our life by the idea of reincarnation, which raises us inwardly above the individual life. As Nietzsche once wished for himself that he might have a 'love of destiny' *(amor fati),* and vowed: 'I will some day be one who says Yes to destiny.' Then his spirit looked in prescience to these heights. But his longing grasped at something which lay beyond his knowing; and so he sank down again into the 'No'. Love of destiny is gained in proportion as we become united with the 'I', which leads us on through one life as we need it to another life as we need it all the more rightly. Love of destiny is possible, if it is at the same time love of one's own higher self. The ancient Indian sought reconciliation with his fate; the ancient Greek strove for freedom from his fate; the Christian endeavoured to resign himself to his fate. But such a resignation can become love which knows, and so may reach its real value. When the light of the wisdom of the spirit that guides us begins to shine in our earthly consciousness, then we begin to feel as if we must rejoice in our destiny.

Future destiny

Till now we have turned our attention to understanding our destiny as it works out of the past into the present. But the thought of reincarnation – if it becomes an active part of our being and not merely an intellectual issue – takes on a special meaning for our future, our task and our endeavour. We will then see how trifling the impetus to personal endeavour was that came from Christianity up till now, and how much force and will-power therefore lay fallow in humanity.

Catholicism has its striving for sanctity, but it is clothed in the garment of merit. It retains the character of compliance with laws or commandments. It lacks insight into a form of human evolution which must be perfected in freedom in stages extending beyond this one life. This is still more lacking in Protestantism, which emphasised 'secular ethics' more and more. But this ethic itself is on the point of collapse because it has lost its metaphysical background; and so only considerations of utility, happiness or custom remain. There are no sure points of view which can lead to the perfecting of humanity, and so in Protestant culture a kind of professional morality stands in the forefront. One has to prove oneself by the demands of life; and religion, where it still finds credence, gives strength for this. After death, marvellous transformations are in store for all, as well as for the individual. These considerations still work on, even among those who have freed themselves from the dogmas of the church, but there is no stronger motive for striving towards personal perfection. Such ideas of the afterlife cripple this striving and the result is that all calls to self-training that emerge unconsciously and instinctively from the will of the age – whether as self-help for health or for business success – come to us in the form of materialistic egotism.

In respect of these considerations, the idea of reincarnation has great significance for humanity. Also all general hopes of development after death that have appeared here and there, are of no importance compared with the living power which lies in a clear and detailed account of human evolution – even if one cannot fully, out of one's personal conviction, agree to all its details.

People who live in the light of the idea of reincarnation know that all their endeavours and even their most secret will have the full value of a reality that works throughout the whole cosmos. They know that this most secret endeavour is important, not only because after death 'all will be laid open' but because the meaning which such a striving has for the future, for their own as well as for the world's future, will be clearly shown forth.

We are not teaching a selfish endeavour after perfecting one's own self. Only misunderstanding, deliberate or unconscious, can thus distort our point of view. Egotism in striving for perfection would – according to the teaching of reincarnation within anthroposophy – be a most dangerous Luciferic temptation, turn someone aside from the divinely willed evolving of the world. To strive after perfection can only be wholesome and work in a wholesome way if it proceeds from free insight into the divine will, if it consists in a reverent receiving of the divine power to help, and in being willing to allow that power to come to full activity: if it aims at producing one who will be a valued fellow-worker in the divine guidance of the world. According to anthroposophical ideas, the striving for perfection is on the right path only if carried on in this sense. Every other representation of it is a misunderstanding if not something worse, and every other method leads astray, leads to corruption. That is why the spiritual edifice of anthroposophy is built up not on directions for self-perfection but on the light it throws upon one's view of the world, out of which each individual can draw the endeavour to strive for perfection in insight and freedom.

One cannot describe the wholesome feeling of fitting into the whole cosmos which one has once such thoughts are admitted into one's mind. Such people are not labouring for the sake of the results, nor for their own well-being, nor for personal holiness; they are building the human being of the future, they are building a future world. A free will has united itself and given itself to a higher will which is striving to the far-off goal of the world.

Even the smallest step they succeed in taking in their meditation is seen to be connected with great spiritual issues. And those who do anything contrary to the divine powers, or even seek to reach their goal without them, are not damned in the medieval sense but are shut out from the divinely willed evolution of the world. Our task is to be active in will, with them and for them. If we are idle, we are only deferring what must happen if we wish to become human beings of the future, and we create new difficulties for ourselves. We do not advance on the way to perfection with a ceaseless and equal pace; the divine powers always take us to their heart, as a mother takes her child when it has made an attempt to walk. Again we are released, with new powers and tasks, and always with the same protection. What we accomplish, not in the full view of others but in the most secret chambers of our heart, bears fruit in the realm of the spirit, for ourselves and for the whole world. But the decisive help for human beings is the divine deed of Christ. Yet they cannot be spared the duty of transforming Christ's help into their own free will. The effect of such an idea can only be felt to be wholesome, in the highest and most spiritual sense.

Suicide and sexuality

Let us turn the light of the thought of reincarnation on two spheres in which humanity today shows its helplessness – suicide, and the question of sex.

Anyone to whom reincarnation seems probable or even only possible will perceive that there is no greater self-deception than for a man to believe he can 'make an end' of his life. Rudolf Steiner described in detail, out of spiritual perception, how such souls suffer after death because of the want of a body which has not done its full service to them; how they suffer under the knowledge that they have made a blunder in a destiny which must now be put to rights, under the knowledge that they have only slunk away from trials which had been assigned to them, and which still remain for them to attempt. This is no external or internal condemnation of the one who has committed suicide, but an agony of soul, whose necessity and reality is placed illuminatingly before us.

Karl Hauptmann saw the essential nature of suicide to lie in this, that one thing in a human being destroys the other things that are in him. Of what use is it when two married people cannot bear one another say to each other, 'It is no use, we must go into another room together; only by doing that can everything come right again!' To commit suicide is just as clever. It is a changing of place: everything else remains. Indeed, many things become worse through the violent change of scene.

The increase in suicide shows, as few other facts do, that the old moral ties are becoming loosened throughout humanity, that new moral forces are necessary if people are to take their earthly activity in full earnestness, and not just as it pleases them to take it. The old church ideas have lost both their terrors and their power to compel. Can we see in the idea of reincarnation a help which is sent to us at the right time? It will not give someone a distaste for suicide merely because it is forbidden by religion and objectionable to morality, but it will allow them to see how the world is fitted together in the course of the divine ordering, and so enable them to form their own resolve in freedom and knowledge.

If a 'league against suicide' were formed to mobilise and concentrate all the old forces against suicide, it would be of little avail if humanity did not have a new power of comprehension. According to the teaching of reincarnation, suicide is the most useless and unreasonable action that someone can take.

The other question facing humanity today is the sexual problem. In the ethical commands and customs of the past, a form of authority speaks to us that does not appeal to modern people. What do they care what other people did, or how they themselves harm or help society? If they ask why, they want quite other reasons in answer. The old morality has gone, humanity is finally losing Moses: even the Moses who still lives on in the Church as a code of morals. One need be neither a canting bigot nor a Philistine when one looks with anxiety to the future of humanity. A young woman said recently, 'The body and its capacity for enjoyment is the only thing we have.' Towards what are we evolving? To a new morality claiming the beautiful words 'truth' and 'freedom'? To depravity? To a return to the old morality?

What has the teaching of reincarnation to say to all this? It does not set up new commandments; it communicates important facts. The true path of humanity leads towards the spirit, and every step forward on this path is bound up with self-discipline. If anyone gives themselves up to the guidance of their bodily lusts, they throw themselves back in their development as a spiritual being. They place acts within the world, which continue to work both upon themselves and upon others. And for everything that has wrought harm, they must one day give compensation; they cannot escape from doing so. Their own being and actions are always of importance for the world. May they see for what they can be responsible! 'For their deeds will follow them' (Rev 14:13).

This has nothing to do with an ascetic smothering of sexuality, although the time will come in the course of human development when sexuality will be laid aside. We are now dealing with the training of humanity's life-forces so that they may be serviceable to the spiritual goal of humanity. The sooner human beings reach this training and the higher their attainments in it, the better for them. Unmastered lusts change in the spiritual land after death into burning fire, and those human spirits that we have forced down to a lower level through our actions also return and demand their due from us. We may not offend the dignity of the spirit. If we see the truth, there remains only, as Plato said, a flight into the good.

The transition in which humanity finds itself today must be clearly recognised. New spiritual laws are replacing former moral laws. People no longer act as they ought, but as they see fit. They no longer listen to a divine will which they do not altogether understand; they perceive a divine world which speaks for itself clearly enough. It is no longer tablets of law but spiritual facts which appear before them and speak to them. Can we fully perceive the entirely different nature of this new thing? Can we recognise it to be a divine word spoken to the age of insight and freedom?

Nietzsche, who felt earlier and more deeply than anyone else the inward situation of humanity in the age of culture, wrote, as is well known, that if religious faith decreased, then people would learn to see themselves as fugitives and inessential, but they would thereby necessarily become weak; they would no longer train themselves in striving and endurance; they would wish for enjoyment in the moment, and would have no more ground for expectation; they would make light of life. Nietzsche's spirit sought anxiously for a 'new influence'. He sought it presciently almost in the right place. In seeking to set up the doctrine of the 'eternal return' or 'eternal recurrence', as a new perception of truth for humanity, so that it might give humanity new inward support, his half-clairvoyant soul had got near, very near to the truth. But the 'eternal recurrence' kills hope and lames one's strength. Reincarnation awakens hope and increases strength. If, instead of his teaching of the 'eternal recurrence' Nietzsche had found that of reincarnation then his two teachings of return and of *Übermensch,* the superman, would not have fallen apart but would have fitted into one another. Reincarnation leads immediately to the service of the superman, but not only to the superman who comes after us, but also to the superman in us.

There are changes, of course, but they are not those which deprive us of our development, not those in which we should lose ourselves. Just as we take ourselves with us into our development, so we take our defects with us also. We cannot cut them off like our hair or our finger-nails. They may be transformed into virtues, but only through development. Life after death is extremely different from our present life, but just because of that, we must remain ourselves, even if we wish only to recognise ourselves.

And so, when we look behind the appearance of the world, we are looking into a noble countenance. In that inner part of the world it is not natural law but moral law that rules. The morality of the world is the foundation upon which we all live. The world is becoming moral, and morality is becoming great. The history of the world is the tribunal which judges the world. This is the world which Kant sought and imagined to be after death. He could not find it in the external world where evil does well and the good does badly, and therefore demanded compensation in the world beyond; in fact for the sake of this compensation he demanded a world beyond. But it was not an *after*world, but a '*behind*-world'. In his day that was certainly a *beyond*, lying beyond the experience of that time. But it is not a matter of a change of place, but of a deeper insight. And when, in reply to Kant, Ludwig Feuerbach asked, 'But who tells us that the universe really corresponds to our demands and wishes?' a half century later the answer came in anthroposophy from behind the appearance of the world itself. From that time on, when looking into the depths of the universe, man is gazing into the countenance of a holy cosmic morality.

So we have a new Moses? Today people still look at the teaching of reincarnation too much with the eyes of Moses. For also in ancient India there was a time of Moses, when reincarnation was seen as a law which made burdensome demands; and that idea is still active among us. When we hear in the Old Testament (Gn 9:6), 'Whoever sheds human blood, by humans shall their blood be shed,' it sounded from the book of cosmic morality, But Moses made a cosmic law into an earthly commandment, and thus he recreated cosmic morality, but on too small a pattern. It was good, but too short. He had not seen and could not see the ultimate truth, that this cosmic morality in its deepest form is cosmic goodness itself. For goodness is not what makes me glad, but what trains me for what is greatest, and so trains me for the greatest of all joys, for sharing in the divine life itself.

It is 'mercy' to be guided upwards. It is 'mercy' to be allowed to make a recompense. It is 'mercy' to grow into unity with the morality of the world. Within the world is a heart that beats for us. This heart sympathises with the highest that is in us, with what is seeking to evolve in us, and out of it, this highest flows to us. It stamps its own nature upon us, as it looks upon us from all sides, and so awakens our own best nature. Only in a world in which a greater 'I' lives, which human beings can recognise as the ultimate wish of their life, only in such a world can they feel at home. The face of Moses is lost in the ray of light which streams from the depths: and out of the inmost place of the cosmos, the Father of the World looks at us through the face of Christ.

Society

Up till now we have looked at man more in himself. Now we will look at the relationship with the community around. How has this relationship to others changed?

In his star aphorisms, Friedrich Nietzsche feels that his friendship with Richard Wagner came out of the firmament. Two stars are drawn to one another out of cosmic spaces, they greet one another as they pass, and hurry away out into cosmic space again. In this great example Nietzsche has realised what every meeting of two people, even their most fleeting meeting, really is. Stars greet one another in passing. According to anthroposophical perception it is true, as old traditions say, that everyone has their star in heaven, and that they are its earthly expression. Everyone a star – yes; everyone a heaven of stars. If one could read in man's deepest nature and destiny, one would see a constellation of stars. The forces working in his life can be written down in the language of the stars. Astrology is today becoming more and more popular in our life, but it comes more out of ancient experience than out of insight, and it is threatened with a dose of the materialism of our age. Through the greater spiritual context of anthroposophy, which tells how, after death, the human being passes through the world of stars and is tested there, we can perceive how these inner realities correspond to the external stars, and then astrology, with purified face, will reveal all the greatness of its mighty conception of the cosmos.

Is it meaningless if I can look at a person in such a way? More sensitive people feel in every conversation that they must know whether the other person is a being which has sprung up out of nothing, fades away again, and, when dying, ceases; or whether that person is a being on whom eternities are working to build it up. In the latter case every turn of conversation becomes different. Our usual conversations merely tickle the soul as they pass, they are unworthy of a human being; and that people do not feel the tragedy of this inadequacy is still more deeply tragic. A vague general hope of immortality is no longer of use. What once lived as a vague feeling that then gradually disappeared comes back to us now as knowledge out of cosmic spaces. What once comforted people as a dogma now seeks to establish itself as a cosmic truth.

Marriage? Where this is more than a love affair made binding at a registry office, or a business transaction, there two souls have been born in the same period of time in order to find one another. The myth of Eros, as Plato tells it in his *Symposium,* is true; only it is more individually true, truer to the 'I', than people could realise in Plato's time. It is not that a man seeks a woman, but that *this* man seeks *this* woman. And the community of life, prepared in higher worlds, is fulfilled on earth. Marriages are made in heaven.

And divorces? Sometimes people have really lived out to the end their destiny together. But woe to them if they too hastily cut the knot they ought to have unloosed. Unfinished and unsettled fates await them and will find them again. Such people will seek one another until they have met and brought what they broke off to a just conclusion.

The real truth which is in a marriage will inevitably come to light through death. Suddenly two people, who have perhaps maintained to the end the lie that they are united in love, will be miles apart. Other marriages again will arise from the deep. If two pieces of electrical apparatus that are tuned to each other can find each other across the whole globe, much more can two human souls who are in harmony. Reincarnation teaches not the indissolubility of marriage, but the deep cosmic seriousness of marriage.

When after his wife's death Thomas Carlyle found in her diary the description of the sorrows of her life at his side, he cried out, 'If I had only five minutes in which to tell her how dearly I loved her!' A deeper conception of the further life, and of reincarnation, could have replied, 'You do not need to wish it, you have her now, and can tell her, and she can hear you. But your wish will also be fulfilled; you will have her again, and will tell her, and she will hear.' Reincarnation is mercy.

Just as humanity at the present time is seeking a new foundation for marriage, so it is also seeking to put the relationship between parents and children upon a new basis. One must not regard children as smaller adults. But the mood which has grown up is one which calls for deeper insight. Our children have not turned up in our home by chance. They have sought us, as we have sought them. Perhaps they were careless in the choice of their parents when they came to live with us; but in any case they have brought with them a large baggage of destiny. They go back just as far as we into the past of humanity, and have, perhaps, sat at the feet of wiser teachers. They bring with them the charge laid upon them by their stars, and it has brought them to life-tasks which lie some decades further on than ours. The teaching we give them can only be a help to development. We cannot decide their development; we can only watch it. Their 'I' carries within it its own mission, and we are the friends of their destiny; all our expectation and pride as adults must be laid aside.

Luther tells us that his teacher always took off his hat when he entered his classroom. 'There might be a mayor, or a councillor, or a doctor among my pupils.' By this one saying that man proved himself a true teacher. His feeling for a truth was much truer than he could then know.

Nations and peoples

From this we turn to the sphere in which at present day there are great struggles and convulsions – to the social question. What form would these struggles take in souls which were filled with thoughts of reincarnation? Epictetus, the Roman slave, told us in what frame of mind he endured the lot of a slave. 'While we live,' he said, 'one man has to play the part of a king, another that of a beggar, but after death they will ask us, as they ask the actors, not, "What part did you play?" but, "How did you play your part?"' Through these words an afterglow from the wisdom of the mysteries still shines.

Yet such stories may awaken the feeling that the teaching of reincarnation is only a new means of keeping the oppressed classes quiet, a new way of pointing to this 'divinely ordained position of dependence'. But what is important here is the difference between the 'I' which is represented and the 'I' which acts that part. If the slave lives in the mood of Epictetus, he may feel himself to be the equal of a king, and, indeed, spiritual investigation shows that, for example, everyone who oppresses a class or a people will in all probability be born again as one of those very people. If I cannot put myself in the place of another, I shall be put in his place; after death, I myself shall find it to be to my own interest to put myself in his place, because in his place I can learn most, and can best atone. After death our desires are changed. The lady who unfeelingly harasses her maid with every mood, increases from day to day the probability that she will wear a servant's dress in her next life. Through a greater sensitivity we are drawn to that place where we think our life may be enriched.

In the past it was said by way of consolation that death makes all men equal. That feeling, which has gradually been forgotten, now comes back to us again as a riper insight. We wander together through our existence for thousands of years. I may probably be meeting the person who is standing before me, not for the first time, probably not for the last. What he outwardly wears is a disguise. His true value may raise him above me, not only inwardly now, but later also outwardly. The king is king for this time, the beggar is now a beggar. Out of such insight into life, if it burns with full power and warmth in the soul, a new deep human feeling must grow. Is not our age, this very age of social study, asking that a more humane humanity be established anew on a more sublime foundation? It is easy to preach this humaneness; it is hard to establish it; without a new deep insight it cannot be maintained, still less brought to life again. Every time we meet anyone, we must look at the person, at the 'I' before us, which is travelling through its incarnations. The world is waiting for a thought, for a truth which will re-establish its humaneness.

Christianity and reincarnation

Someone may object that a new basis is more necessary for our relationship to humanity and its life on earth than for our relationship to individuals. Why has traditional Christianity failed when faced with social questions? Why can it only preach morality? Because it has not had the greatest thoughts about the life of human beings on earth and for their work on earth. It spoke only about doing our duty in our calling, about thankfulness to God and about helping others. But human beings must see the positive meaning of their earthly work if they are to apply themselves to it with their best powers. 'Remain true to the earth, my brothers!' was Nietzsche's saying in condemnation of the mood which turned people away from the earth. Nietzsche expressed the wish of a whole age, as it felt the failure of its religious ideas, and looked for new light upon its earthly task.

In the light of the thought of reincarnation our work on earth appears quite new. We have not been thrown by chance by the waves upon the shore of this world, to get on as best we can until the ship calls to take us home again. We are *the* earthly race, united to our earthly home until it becomes a ruin. Together we have to struggle to gain for the spirit from the earth that which we can gain from it alone. No godlike race can do this without man. We are working not only for our children, we are working for ourselves; we are working for the whole future of the human race, of which we ourselves are members, when we bring forth into the light of day all earth's possibilities, when we impress upon the earth her divine meaning – the meaning which man alone can find. Nothing is lost which happens upon earth for the sake of the life of humanity; it happens for us, it happens also for the future of the spirit itself. Only when we have perfected the earth may we hope to take leave of it, and look for a 'new earth'. Then the earth, and man too, will become spiritual; but it will become spiritual – as man will – with the results of all the work done on earth during all the thousands of years.

So our view of humanity becomes ever broader and greater. The barriers break down between peoples as well as between classes. Externally they are overthrown by the modern communications, by telephone, by radio and cinema. Inwardly they are breaking down through the idea of reincarnation.

If it is we ourselves who pass on through different nations, what is left of national fanaticism?

Then is our connection with our own nation destroyed by the teaching of reincarnation? Does a nation not require all the love of its people, which ought not to flee from it, either as capital or as ideas? Do we not rather need a new spiritual basis for a true love of one's nation so that we may be raised above natural tribal feeling and above false racial passions? But this thought brings again the idea of reincarnation. 'My people' is the community of my destiny in this earthly life. The folk-soul is fumbling after a newer, deeper basis for such a community of destiny. Not by the blindness of natural law have I been thrown upon this place of earth. I have sought this nation, not only because I wished to learn something in it, not only because I wished to help it, but because my soul itself is related to it, my soul, and not only my body. To disavow my nation and its destiny is to disavow myself. Certainly the destiny of my people may be to suffer need; yet the task of this people may be spiritual. I must seek not any political delusion, but the inward meaning of my connection with my nation. Here my earthly task awaits me; here must I fulfil it.

Thought about one's race, is full of materialism; it makes one blind and arrogant from pride in one's inheritance, and arrogant because of one's descent; it changes peoples into beasts of prey, which tear one another. One can already hear the voices of these beasts of prey, for example, in Oswald Spengler's new book, *The Decline of the West*. We have dire need of a new basis for an alliance of all peoples, an alliance which at the same time leaves us free as human beings.

For the thoughts of humanity are now going beyond individual nations. We disavow the essential side of our Germanic nature when we try to kill this thought in us. Isolde Kurz once described impressively in a poem how

Scipio, the Conqueror of Carthage, after the great success of his life, knocks at heaven's gate. He expects that the greatness of his deeds will infallibly find recognition. But the thoughts of the powers which guide the destinies of mankind are higher. What he did was necessary and great, but he lacked one thing: 'You do not know the feelings of an oppressed nation; be born again as a Punic slave!' What if the poetess had known that the investigations of Rudolf Steiner showed that someone who inflicts misery upon a people will, in all probability, have to live his next life among these very people? Let us imagine that a prophet had appeared among the men of Versailles in 1919 and told them this, and that he had succeeded not only in convincing their minds fully of it, but also in making it part of their inmost feelings. The anxiety they would then have had for their own future, even if it had not immediately taken form as a political action, can show us the significance which the idea of reincarnation may have for the future of humanity. And that of which we are speaking would only be the first egotistic reactions, and not yet the delicate action of the spirit.

The greatest benefit humanity could receive today would be a spiritual view, which included the national (not the nationalistic) and the super-national (not the international), and which gave to both, their due rights. Unless this spiritual point of view comes to life in humanity – it need only be the knowledge of the few and the surmise of the many – then humanity is going towards newer and more dangerous catastrophes, in spite of, or just because of, national enthusiasms. The ancient thoughts of Christianity and humanism are united today with new knowledge. Every folk-soul has its mission. But man on his earthly way passes through the peoples. Just as children have sought their parents, so individuals have sought the nation which can help them and which they can help. By this, and not by any naturalistic hereditary unity of nation, is our love of our nation explained. It is only the unspiritual man who can fear that the ennobling of the tree will rob it of its life-force. It is not love of our nation to draw that love from any other source than from the spirit. And every man can see that the racial theories are only a helpless search for such a spiritual source.

New eyes must be opened to see not only our own nation, but all nations. The ancient Christian love of one's enemy is falling into ruin, and Christian circles are foremost in the work of pulling it down. Elementary feelings are furbished up as Christian. 'If Christianity demands of me a love of the French, then I give up my Christianity here and now!' I have myself heard sayings like this, which was uttered by a highly educated woman, from the lips of princes of the Church. But Christian love of one's enemy must not only be freed from all sentimentality, it must also be raised above everything that is of the nature of a commandment, or is simply a matter of the feelings. The 'simple' announcement that God created all human beings, and Christ died for all, is no longer sufficient. This is not only seen among humanity in general, but also in Protestant circles. Mankind's community of destiny in its unity and in its individual parts must be freshly perceived. We live in the nation – we pass through the nations. I fulfil the intention of my destiny only when I accomplish my task for my nation; and only when I look beyond my nation to humanity do I grasp the aim of the earth. We cannot free ourselves from this twofold attitude to life, and it is out of this attitude only that we can work out salvation for our own nation, and yet not only for our own nation.

The old view taken by western Christianity is being subjected to an overpoweringly severe strain. More and more people stream through the gate of birth, into existence. How about them? The problem was always there, but we did not see it; we could always withdraw from it into our own private dwelling. Now, however, such questions surround us like high mountains. Where are all these people heading? A sergeant in the army remarked to me, 'In heaven there'll be no room for all these people who are constantly being born upon the earth.' The idealist, trained in philosophy, expresses himself differently: 'That there is a God I can still believe; but that the single individual is so valuable to this God that he continues after death, I can no longer believe.' The pious Christian can only cast such questions hopefully upon the incomprehensibility of God, which would not be incomprehensible if all these questions did not find room for themselves in it. In all cases of difficulty he brings up his 'confidence in faith'. At least the question, 'What will become of all the people who have not known Christ in this life?' was raised in a circle of friends by one such Christian, only to cast it upon God's incomprehensibility. Do we not see that these ancient opinions simply do not touch humanity and its problems any longer?

And now the knowledge of reincarnation comes and says, 'You deceive yourselves when you think that new people are for ever coming up out of nothing. Humanity strives together out of the dark into the light. It is a closed fellowship with a common destiny. It has existed for thousands of years, and it will continue to exist for thousands of years longer. We are a single, great people, and have been permitted to leave the kingdoms of divine creation, and are now wandering together through the desert.' Those who can bring this thought to life within themselves feel as if for the first time *one* humanity existed for him. We must not accept every aspect of humans as essentially human, but behind the human appearance a human 'I' lives that is laboriously seeking its way towards the heights of humanity. Wherever a human heart beats lives a member of this great community of those who are united by human destiny, to whom the earth is entrusted and who are entrusted to the earth. Our human dignity is not ours through this one birth, but we have borne it for thousands of years in our 'I' – not in our body – in spite of our strayings from the goal of humanity.

When we look back into the past, Christian Morgenstern said, 'Why do we always speak of "*the* ancient Indians or Egyptians"? Why do we not speak of "*We* ancient Indians or Egyptians"?' The destiny of the past is our destiny also; it is within us and makes us understand. New light plays upon a hundred questions, not only on the question of pious people, 'What becomes of people who did not come to know Christ in this life?' but also on thoughtful doubts, 'What is the meaning of the fact that in great catastrophes thousands of people perish?' Here, Rudolf Steiner's investigations were equally illuminating, Through the shock of death especial powers are awakened in man. By common perishing, fellowships of a common destiny were formed, to which a common future task could be entrusted. Providence and predestination are found extending far forward in this plan. Even the hopeless work of standing all day by machines, the sorrowful slavery to mechanism which exists in industry today, has its significance. People who today are tragically exploited as workers bear within them a hidden seed, and the future of humanity will one day be decisively carried on by the hidden forces which are formed in such lives.

Conclusion

After all that has been said, it cannot be thought to be a rhetorical phrase, but rather an important deduction drawn from our study of the life of our times, if we conclude with the following words. It is a great moment when the idea of reincarnation enters the west anew. It is no longer a mountainous weight of reincarnation, such as it was when it oppressed India, but a light of reincarnation which illuminates all the spheres of life.

The teaching of reincarnation as it appears now has taken into itself the results of the evolution of western Christian culture. In this western culture with the ideas of evolution, reincarnation is brought no longer as an endless returning but as an unending ascent. In this Christian culture with its message of mercy, reincarnation no longer looks at human beings through the eyes of a judge, but through the eyes of a teacher – indeed, through the eyes of the Redeemer. A healing and holy ordering of the world – in which cosmic goodness as revealed in Christ – diligently leads humanity upwards. The teaching of reincarnation has never appeared in this form until now; it has never yet spoken to humanity with this voice; it has never looked upon humanity through such eyes.

Humanity's inward need is craving for new thoughts which can bear it up; but often before, such implored-for thoughts have been here and have not been recognised. The author of this book is convinced that hope for humanity lies only in Christ. But through the thought of reincarnation Christianity puts on a new appearance, and through Christianity reincarnation assumes its true appearance. It is of immense importance today that the teaching of reincarnation should appear in a Christian spirit.

This too, was Rudolf Steiner's endeavour. And the author of this book regards it as a service which he has to render to humanity in a serious hour of its destiny, that he should help people to take this teaching seriously, to think it through, to live with it, and to take it up.

Index

Meditation
Guidance of the Inner Life

Friedrich Rittelmeyer

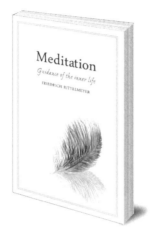

The demands of modern life are such that many people find great value in meditation. It can be hard to know where to start, however, or how to progress.

In this classic work, Friedrich Rittelmeyer recognises the difficulties we face and proposes a Christian meditative path, to guide and inspire. His work is based on the Gospel of St John and he shows how the imagery in the text can be brought alive in people's hearts through thought and imagination.

Rittelmeyer's inner training is presented with a wealth of practical advice, and a gentle trust in his reader which glows from every page.

florisbooks.co.uk

Rudolf Steiner
Enters My Life

Friedrich Rittelmeyer

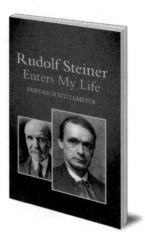

Born in southern Germany in 1872, Friedrich Rittelmeyer was a leading figure in the Lutheran church at the beginning of the twentieth century. His was an influential pulpit, and he was a pioneer of a new meditative approach, seeking to re-establish the relevance of the Gospels.

His life took an unexpected turn when, in 1911, he encountered Rudolf Steiner for the first time. He spent the next ten years critically appraising and investigating Steiner's ideas. This book is a fascinating and insightful autobiographical account of those years, as well a rigorous scrutiny of anthroposophy.

florisbooks.co.uk

Christianity and Reincarnation

Rudolf Frieling

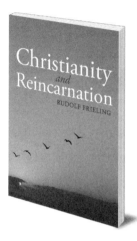

In this challenging book, Rudolf Frieling makes the case for the integration of reincarnation into a Christian world view.

He shows how an esoteric Christianity was brought to life again through the thinking of Rudolf Steiner, arguing that theology around the 'end of days' has shown how a gap exists between death and resurrection on the Last Day.

Presenting the essence of Christianity, Frieling shows how it harmonises with reincarnation, and examines the relationship of reincarnation to the Bible.

florisbooks.co.uk

Floris
Books

For news on all our **latest books,**
and to receive **exclusive discounts,**
join our mailing list at:

florisbooks.co.uk

Plus subscribers get a FREE book
with every online order!